Healthy Babies

food for healthy babies & toddlers

THE AUSTRALIAN

Women's Weekly

contents

As a mother, and now a grandmother, I understand the concern parents feel when it's time to give baby their first food. Often, it doesn't get any easier feeding and pleasing toddlers and pre-schoolers either. This book is full of information, recipes and tips – all with a healthy slant – to guide you through these stages. It's reassuring to know that kids' taste buds develop and change as they grow; offer them small amounts of a variety of food often, and all will be well.

Pamela Clark

Food director

Foundations for Life

Every baby is different

From day one, issues around feeding your baby will become a serious preoccupation. Indeed, together with lack of sleep, feeding is an area that creates major anxiety for parents. Whether you are offering the breast or the bottle, it's natural to be totally focused on the feeding habits of your baby. Many mums find themselves fervently watching the clock in order to discover some meaning or some semblance of a pattern in the sleeping/feeding/playing routines of their babies. Of course, the thing we all discover is that there are no strict patterns and it's unwise to get too regimented in your thinking because every baby's needs are different and their tastes and habits are forever changing. This is the ongoing feature of a child's relationship to food: their eating habits will constantly change. Babies who fed voraciously for the first six months might become picky eaters once they start on solids. Babies who began life as delicate little eaters can develop big appetites. For parents, the child/food relationship can be a source of frustration. When you have a robust 12-month-old seemingly living on air, it's natural to feel anxious. It's also natural to feel like throwing your lovingly created meal against the wall when your little angel rejects it. We've all been there. The key is to try to relax and trust that it could all be a different story next week.

body building Everything your baby eats is building every cell in his body. So it stands to reason that the better and healthier his food, the better and healthier his body. Give him the best possible start in life with fresh, healthy food.

Familiar questions

Will you be able to sustain breastfeeding or will you use a bottle? How often should you be feeding? How much milk is enough? When do you introduce solids? What are the best foods to start with? And how can you ensure your child gets a nutritionally balanced diet?

Questions about food and diet will constantly surface throughout your child's life. At every point, it's important to try to stay calm, trust your instincts and resist the urge to compare your child with other children at playgroup. Trust that you will find the answers that are right for you and your child. This book is designed to help you find that confidence to make healthy choices for your family.

A WORD ON SALT We have checked the sodium levels in our recipes, they all come in under the recommended guidelines. Salt does draw out and emphasise flavours in food, but immature palates shouldn't be exposed to salty food, in fact, excess salt can be harmful to children's underdeveloped organs. When you're using commercially-made products such as sauces, stocks etc, use as many salt-reduced or salt-free products as you can to lower the recipe's sodium levels even more.

Don't rush things

In previous generations, mothers were encouraged to start their babies on solid foods at a very young age, in some cases when they were as tiny as six weeks, when their little digestive systems were not ready to cope. These days, the advice from doctors and health professionals is to wait until your baby is at least four months old before introducing solids. In fact, paediatric hospitals around Australia strongly recommend holding off on the introduction of solids until six months, especially if there is a history of allergies, asthma or food intolerances in your family. If you're worried about when to start your baby on solids, talk to your doctor or local baby health nurse. You may face scrutiny and pressure from well-meaning family members who suggest starting solids early to 'help the baby sleep through' or to satisfy a big baby, but there is little evidence to suggest that starting solids earlier helps in these situations. Mother's milk – or infant formula – provides all the calories and nourishment required by your baby until at least four months, and there are no advantages in offering solid food any earlier.

Somewhere between four and six months, babies will also show signs of readiness to eat solid foods: they'll start to put things in their mouths, they'll be hungry and wanting more frequent feeds, they'll be interested in watching you eat, and they'll be trying to grab the food you're eating. Another sign of readiness is the ability to sit upright when gently supported: babies need to have good control of the head and neck (essential for safe swallowing) before they can embark on solid foods.

Fussy toddlers? Focus on quality not quantity

Many parents worry about whether their toddlers are eating enough. Sometimes, it can feel like most of the food ends up on the bib or the floor. Often, the foods they tried and liked last week won't pass muster this week. It can be exasperating. But don't worry: babies are good at self regulating and they won't let themselves go hungry. You can offer your baby the food, but you can't force her to eat it. So long as you are offering a range of healthy foods within a happy and loving environment, you can be confident that she won't be missing out.

After 12 months a baby's growth rate slows down and they are not as hungry as they previously may have been. So, while you might think they would need copious amounts of food to give them energy for their increased activity and mobility, rest assured their little bodies can function very efficiently even when they appear to eat small amounts.

Grazing is good

Many toddlers and pre-schoolers prefer to graze rather than consume three large meals a day. They also tend to be unpredictable: one day they will be asking for seconds and the next day they'll be playing with their food. If they don't eat a huge amount at one meal, don't fret. The key is to consider how much food they have consumed in a 24-hour period: the slices of cheese, the bites of ham, the yogurt, the banana, the half-eaten sandwich and other mouthfuls of food all count. Chances are they will have consumed a perfectly healthy amount of diverse foods over that time. Also look at the indicators of general well-being: is your child happy and active, with overall good health (including weight gain)? These are the things that matter rather than the quantity of food they eat. If you are worried that your baby is not putting on weight, you should see your doctor who might suggest that you visit a dietician.

no sugar Don't give your baby sugar. She doesn't need it and it could damage her developing teeth – she'll get plenty of natural sugar from fruit; try mixing pureed fruit into natural yogurt.

Finger food: the road to independence

Babies and toddlers are hard-wired to exercise and express their independence, and they all reach a point – at around nine months, when they gain enough finger control – when they want to feed themselves. Finger food is perfect for them. Strips of steamed vegetables, ripe and cooked fruit (melons, pear and banana are ideal), slices of cheese or grated cheese, cooked shell pasta, finger sandwiches, finely sliced cooked meats and plain biscuits are all good places to start.

Even without teeth, many babies can chew effectively by around eight or nine months of age. It's important to encourage chewing to assist with the development of the muscles essential for eating and speech. Once your baby starts teething, it opens up the dietary possibilities even further. Entice them by placing a range of differently coloured foods on the plate. Make sure you praise your child for eating a range of foods rather than focusing on the quantity of food they eat.

VARIETY IS THE SPICE OF LIFE

While they're called 'solids', a baby's first foods are actually very sloppy. When you do start introducing solids, you should begin with rice cereal made to a semi-liquid consistency. After a few weeks of rice cereal, you can progress to foods like pureed vegetables (such as pumpkin, potato, carrot and zucchini), pureed stewed fruits (pears and apples are good), mashed ripe bananas and full-cream yogurt. These first 'solid' foods need to be smooth in texture and mild in taste. At this stage, you're offering 'tastes' for your baby, so begin slowly and introduce new flavours gradually, one at a time (every three days or so) so you can monitor your baby's reaction to the food.

After several weeks of eating different fruits and vegetables, you can gradually change the texture of the foods from a smooth puree to a mashed texture to encourage chewing. At seven to eight months you can also start introducing more foods with a higher protein and iron content and a thicker texture – such as well-cooked meat, chicken or fish – blended with the vegetables. You could also try blending some lentils or baked beans or introducing some wheat-based cereals such as couscous and pasta before moving onto finger foods.

Introducing your baby to new foods is an exciting, fun and messy time. Make sure you have a good supply of large bibs and facecloths at the ready and try to relax about the mess and potential food refusal. Remember, your aim is to make mealtimes enjoyable, not a battleground.

If your baby is enjoying the new foods then keep introducing new flavours. You can also start giving your baby small tastes (blended at first) of the foods you are eating for dinner when they're suitable. These are the baby steps to incorporating your baby into communal family dinners.

Reverse the trend Latest figures show that around 20 to 25 per cent of Australian children are overweight or obese and this percentage is increasing. Studies also show that once a child or adolescent is obese or overweight, they are unlikely to reduce it as an adult. These alarming trends can be attributed to growing numbers of children eating the wrong foods and not doing enough daily exercise. You can give your child a wonderful start in life by offering them only healthy foods while they're young. By the time they're old enough to be making decisions for themselves, they'll instinctively choose to eat a healthy diet.

Choking hazards While it's exciting to expose your child's palate to new flavours and textures, and see the delight they bring, you have to be on your guard for potential choking hazards. Hard fruits and vegetables such as raw apples, carrots and celery are high-risk foods for babies and toddlers. It is recommended that whole apples and carrots are not given until a child is four years of age. Whole nuts also should be avoided until children are five years of age. Mandarin segments and whole grapes are also hazardous: they need to be cut in half. And the golden rule is to supervise your baby every mealtime: don't let him walk around while eating and be very watchful if you give him snacks in the car.

Tips on food hygiene

- Make sure you wash your hands before preparing or handling food for your baby.
- For the first 12 months, all of your baby's milk bottles and any other containers used for storing milk must be sterilised in a bottle steriliser (or in boiling water on the stove) after every use.
- Wash your toddler's hands before every meal.
- Always prepare your food on a clean chopping board washed with hot water.
- You can freeze your pureed fruits and vegetables in ice-cube trays or plastic containers. Wash the containers in hot soapy water and rinse well (alternatively use a microwaveable bottle steriliser) before filling with food.
- Wash all of your baby's cups, plates, forks and spoons in hot soapy water or a dishwasher after every use.

Allergy alert Over the past two decades, there has been an increase in the incidence of food allergies, asthma and eczema in young children aged between 0 and 5. The foods that are most commonly associated with causing allergic reactions are milk, egg, peanuts, shellfish, fish, sesame and soy. Be wary of all of these food allergens and introduce them slowly. Peanut and other nut products shouldn't be introduced before 12 months. Children with a strong family history of food allergy should avoid all peanut products until after 3 years of age. Strawberries can also cause severe reactions in some children, while honey has been known to cause botulism and egg white may contain harmful bacteria, so these should be avoided for the first 12 months.

toddler treats Don't deprive your toddler of all treats – an Easter egg hunt, for example, is something he'll remember with pleasure and, as it only happens once a year, it won't do any harm.

AVOID JUNK FOOD

High sugar, high-fat foods such as soft drinks, sweets and chips contain no nutritional value and are unnecessary in a young child's diet. Sugary drinks such as cordial and soft drinks are detrimental because they contain sugar, caffeine and chemicals that are totally unsuitable for your baby's digestive system. Fruit juices, too, are high in sugar and should be avoided. Milk and water are the best drinks to offer.

It's also important to protect your baby's new teeth, so avoid cakes smothered in icing, lollies, sweet biscuits and flavoured milks. And never give juice in a bottle of any type at bedtime: putting a baby to bed with a bottle to suck is very harmful to teeth. Your babies and toddlers don't know these foods and drinks exist, so why introduce them? They won't feel deprived if they are not included in their diet and they don't see you eating them. They'll learn about these foods soon enough via television advertising and their peers at school – and the best defence against this inevitable intrusion is to have established their taste for fresh, healthy foods from an early age.

Healthy foods are needed throughout life. By making family meals healthy and nutritious, you are setting an example for your baby and toddler to follow, fostering an understanding of the importance of good food and encouraging their preferences for healthy choices later in life.

Equipment Needed

Here's a basic checklist of the equipment needed for feeding your babies and toddlers:

- A supply of baby bottles and matching teats. It's best to have a range of bottles with different capacities and measurements clearly marked on the side. If you're breast-feeding and you intend to express your milk, you'll need around three bottles for storing the milk. If you're bottle-feeding, you'll need around six bottles.
- A few soft-edged spoons: there are purpose-designed plastic spoons available from supermarkets that are perfect.
- Unbreakable plates and bowls.
- A fork or potato masher (to mash vegetables to a semi-smooth consistency).
- Hand-held blender or food processor (to help you attain the smooth consistency that most young babies require).
- A collection of small plastic containers with lids for storing leftovers in the refrigerator and for freezing freshly cooked batches of vegetables.
- A high chair: it's often more comfortable to sit your baby on your lap when you start feeding, but you'll soon need to transfer to a high chair.
- A good supply of bibs, facecloths and mopping up cloths.

breast or bottle

The immediate question you face after the birth of your baby is whether you will breastfeed or bottle-feed and the answer will depend on a number of factors including your birthing experience, your philosophies on baby care, your previous breastfeeding experiences and the emotional support you receive in those vital first few weeks after the birth.

breast milk vs formula

Breast milk is nature's perfect food for babies and comes conveniently packaged. It contains all your baby's nutritional needs: it's easy to digest and is served on tap, whenever required, at just the right temperature, in a warm, hygienic environment. It also contains antibodies against illness and optimises brain growth and development.

The advantages are compelling and it would seem that breast milk is the most natural choice a mother (and baby) could make. Yet, while breastfeeding is the most natural thing in the world, it is not always easy. In fact, for some women, it can be very hard. In the midst of the upheaval that comes with bringing home a new baby, breastfeeding difficulties can cause anguish for mums and distress for babies. Sometimes, breastfeeding just cannot be sustained.

If this is the case and you are bottle-feeding your baby, you can take comfort in the knowledge that today's infant formulas are a reliable option, offering the closest thing that science can create to mothers' milk. These formulas are manufactured to very strict standards and they will meet all your baby's nutritional needs.

Whether you breastfeed or bottle-feed, your baby will exist on a milk diet for the first four to six months, at which time you can start introducing solids. (The official World Health Organization guidelines recommend a milk-only diet for the first six months; in Australia, the prevailing medical advice allows for some flexibility, recommending milk feeds for around six months and at least four months). Cow's milk is not suitable for infants under 12 months of age.

hint Don't struggle alone. Lactation consultants, child-care nurses, nursing mothers' associations and the breast feeding advice line are all there to help.

Feeding is bonding

Whether you are breastfeeding or bottle-feeding, the important thing to remember is that each time you sit down to feed, you're fulfilling your baby's emotional as well as nutritional needs. New babies do not have very good vision, but their sight is able to focus on a distance of between 20cm and 30cm, the all-important distance between their face and yours when you cradle them in your arms for feeding. That is no accident – it is a profoundly unforgettable moment of connection when your baby fixes his gaze firmly on your face and looks into your eyes, drunk on the bliss of a full tummy.

Feeding times play a special role in creating intimacy between you and your child, and all the chaos created by this new little addition to the household can be (and should be) forgotten while you both share this special bond.

Ideally, at least initially, try to feed in the same location every time. Choose a comfortable chair in a quiet part of the house where you can relax and give your newborn your full attention. Feeding is an integral part of mothering and is a deeply satisfying time for both of you.

For breastfeeding mums

Many women can establish breastfeeding smoothly from day one, but for many others it takes perseverance and for some it can be a lengthy and emotional process. There can be struggles over the baby's attachment, discomfort from cracked, sore nipples and the pain of mastitis. It's also common for new mums to feel anxious that they're not producing enough milk, but this is rarely the case: it's more likely that baby is not feeding efficiently and needs help attaching. Signs to gauge if baby is taking enough food include, six to eight wet nappies a day, two or more poos, weight gain and a baby who is alert and wants to feed. It's worth remembering that:

- Successful breastfeeding is a skill mothers and babies have to learn, requiring patience, practice, and position. Once your baby is correctly positioned, and sucks well, feeding should not hurt and milk should flow smoothly.
- Breastfeeding for 6 months is a great start in life. Continuing to 12 months delivers a range of long-term benefits to your child, reducing the chance of asthma and eczema, heart disease, juvenile diabetes and even obesity.
- Establish your own feeding routine. There are no rules regarding the duration of each breastfeed. Some babies are fast drinkers, some are slower.
- Make sure your baby empties the breast, taking in both the protein-rich foremilk (the milk at the beginning of the feed) and the richer, creamier hind milk (the milk that flows as the breast is emptied). The hind milk is high in kilojoules and fat, which are essential to baby's growth and development. Emptying the breast will also ensure against mastitis. Early childhood experts recommend offering both breasts at each feed. If baby doesn't take much from the second breast, then commence the next feed on that breast.

If you are bottle-feeding

Women turn to bottle-feeding for many reasons. In some cases, breastfeeding is just too difficult to establish and so bottle-feeding is the best option; rest assured this is a reliable alternative that will not hinder your child's health or development. Sometimes, there are feelings of sadness or guilt associated with bottle-feeding, but don't punish yourself. The best thing you can do for your child is to look after yourself: and that means relaxing in the knowledge that you are doing the best you possibly can for your baby. There are many other issues that you will face as a parent, and this is not one to fret about. And any breast milk that you have managed to give your baby, no matter how little, has been beneficial.

All infant formulas on the market are comparable and have to meet strict government standards. Variations in price do not reflect quality or nutritional value, so you can choose the brand that suits your budget. Formulas labelled 'from birth' are for newborns and are suitable up to the age of 12 months. Those labelled 'follow on' formulas are fortified with iron, protein and other minerals and are not suitable for babies under six months. Bottle-feeding requires a lot of stringent hygiene control, and constant washing and sterilising of equipment. While you can boil everything together in a large saucepan, it is worth investing in a microwaveable sterilising unit or an anti-bacterial solution. If bottle-feeding, remember:

- Optimise the bonding process by holding your baby close to your chest, as if you are breastfeeding. You can talk and sing quietly while you're feeding, which will help teach your baby communication skills.
- Most babies like the formula at room temperature: the best method is to place the bottle in a jug of boiled water. Microwaving can overheat the milk.
- The pleasure of connecting with your baby on this intimate level is something dads and other family members can share.
- Exhausted mums can take a rest while someone else takes care of the baby.

Weaning from the breast

Weaning means you stop breastfeeding and replace these feeds with other sustenance: for babies younger than six months this means replacing it with formula; for older babies it means replacing it with a combination of solid food, formula and/or water.

■ The time to wean is when it feels right for you and your baby or when circumstances make it necessary.

■ Weaning from the breast should be a gradual process: begin by eliminating one breastfeed a day, replacing it with a formula feed. Then, after a week, drop another daily breastfeed and so on.

■ If you stop breastfeeding before your baby is seven or eight months old, you will need to wean onto a bottle with a teat. Babies eight months and older can usually make the transition to a sippy cup. Remember, cow's milk is not suitable for children younger than 12 months.

■ Many breastfeeding mums returning to work opt to combine bottle-feeding with breastfeeding. This means they can still maintain the morning and evening breastfeeds while the daytime carer gives the bottle feeds. This combination can work very effectively.

■ For help with weaning, contact your local early childhood health nurse.

Wonder and bewilderment

The arrival of a baby is a joyful, much-anticipated occasion. But that's not to overlook that caring for these tiny humans is an energy-zapping job that is challenging and demanding. Whether you are breastfeeding or bottle-feeding, the first 6-8 weeks of your baby's life can be bewildering and very stressful, especially for first-time parents. New babies don't know the difference between night and day: it's just a rolling 24-hour cycle of sleeps and feeds. Feeding every couple of hours around the clock is physically and mentally exhausting. You have every reason to feel fragile.

Things should settle down a little after 6 weeks, but if you still seem to be feeding non-stop, contact your local early childhood health nurse who can provide invaluable help and information for managing those sleepless nights.

The introduction of solids (at any time from 4-6 months) can be another confusing time as you both adjust to the new routine of three daytime 'meals' with the milk becoming an accompaniment rather than the main meal. Whether you are breastfeeding or bottle-feeding, the key is to make it a gradual process to allow you both to adjust to the changes.

THE LOGISTICS OF BOTTLE-FEEDING

■ Bottle-feeding requires an outlay on bottles, teats, sterilising equipment and the ongoing costs of the formula. You'll need six bottles and matching teats.

■ You'll need to disinfect your baby's bottles for the first 12 months of his life while his immune system is still immature.

■ Everything used to feed your baby must be sterilised after every use. Wash first in hot soapy water, then rinse in hot water and place on clean paper towel to dry before sterilising.

■ When preparing formula, always use the correct proportion of scoops per millilitre of water, as per instructions. Have a supply of pre-boiled water (in sealed, sterile bottles) on hand at all times.

■ When you go out, take a supply of pre-boiled water and powdered formula in separate containers and mix them when required.

first foods

Make and freeze purees in ice-block containers. Introduce your baby gradually to a variety of flavours and textures, mild and smooth to start with, gradually moving to slightly stronger-flavoured food with more texture.

....

avocado and cucumber puree

1 large ripe avocado (320g), chopped coarsely

1 lebanese cucumber (130g), peeled, seeded, chopped coarsely

1 Blend or process ingredients until smooth.

prep time 5 minutes makes 1 cup

nutritional count per tablespoon 4.2g total fat (0.9g saturated fat); 171kJ (41 cal); 0.2g carbohydrate; 0.4g protein; 0.4g fibre

tip This puree is not
suitable to freeze; it will
discolour when thawed.

cauliflower, broccoli and cheese puree

100g cauliflower, chopped coarsely
150g broccoli, chopped coarsely
¼ cup (30g) coarsely grated cheddar cheese
2 tablespoons water

1 Steam vegetables until tender; drain.
2 Blend or process vegetables, cheese and the water
until smooth. Push through sieve into small bowl.
prep + cook time 20 minutes **makes** ¾ cup
nutritional count per tablespoon 1.2g total fat
(0.7g saturated fat); 79kJ (19 cal); 0.3g carbohydrate;
1.6g protein; 0.6g fibre

potato, kumara and parsnip puree

1 small kumara (250g), chopped coarsely
1 small potato (120g), chopped coarsely
1 small parsnip (120g), chopped coarsely
1 tablespoon water

1 Steam vegetables until tender; drain.
2 Push vegetables through sieve into small bowl;
stir in the water.
prep + cook time 30 minutes **makes** 1 cup
nutritional count per tablespoon 0g total fat
(0g saturated fat); 96kJ (23 cal); 4.5g carbohydrate;
0.7g protein; 0.7g fibre

dhal puree

¾ cup (180ml) water
200g pumpkin, chopped coarsely
1 small carrot (70g), chopped coarsely
1 small zucchini (90g), chopped coarsely
2 tablespoons red lentils

1 Combine ingredients in small saucepan; bring
to the boil. Reduce heat; simmer, uncovered, about
15 minutes or until vegetables and lentils are tender.
2 Blend or process mixture until smooth. Push
through sieve into small bowl.
prep + cook time 25 minutes **makes** 1 cup
nutritional count per tablespoon 0.1g total fat
(0g saturated fat); 67kJ (16 cal); 2.2g carbohydrate;
0g protein; 0.8g fibre

chicken, corn and risoni puree

100g chicken breast fillet, chopped coarsely
1¼ cups (310ml) water
1 cup (160g) fresh or frozen corn kernels
1 tablespoon risoni pasta

1 Combine ingredients in small saucepan; bring
to the boil. Reduce heat; simmer, uncovered, about
10 minutes or until pasta is tender and chicken
is cooked through.
2 Blend or process mixture until smooth. Push
through sieve into small bowl.
prep + cook time 25 minutes **makes** 1 cup
nutritional count per tablespoon 0.7g total fat
(0.2g saturated fat); 159kJ (38 cal); 4.7g carbohydrate;
2.8g protein; 0.7g fibre
tip If using fresh kernels, you will need about
1 trimmed corn cob (250g) for this recipe.

cauliflower, broccoli and cheese puree

potato, kumara and parsnip puree

dhal puree

chicken, corn and risoni puree

ratatouille puree

veal mince and bean puree

fish chowder puree

carrot and broccolini puree

ratatouille puree

2 teaspoons olive oil

1 large zucchini (150g), chopped coarsely

1 baby eggplant (60g), chopped coarsely

½ cup (130g) bottled tomato pasta sauce

2 tablespoons water

2 fresh basil leaves

1 Heat oil in medium saucepan; cook zucchini and
eggplant, stirring, 5 minutes. Add sauce and the water;
bring to the boil. Reduce heat; simmer, covered, about
15 minutes or until vegetables soften.

2 Blend or process tomato mixture with basil
until smooth. Push through sieve into small bowl.

prep + cook time 25 minutes **makes** 1 cup

nutritional count per tablespoon 0.9g total fat
(0.1g saturated fat); 67kJ (16 cal); 1.4g carbohydrate;
0.4g protein; 0.5g fibre

veal mince and bean puree

1 teaspoon olive oil

120g veal mince

½ cup (130g) bottled tomato pasta sauce

¼ cup (50g) rinsed, drained, canned butter beans

3 fresh flat leaf parsley sprigs

1 tablespoon water

1 Heat oil in small frying pan; cook mince, stirring,
about 5 minutes or until cooked through. Add sauce;
bring to the boil. Reduce heat; simmer, uncovered,
about 3 minutes or until mixture is thickened.

2 Blend or process veal mixture and remaining ingredients
until smooth. Push through sieve into small bowl.

prep + cook time 15 minutes **makes** 1 cup

nutritional count per tablespoon 1.2g total fat
(0.3g saturated fat); 105kJ (25 cal); 1.1g carbohydrate;
2.4g protein; 0.3g fibre

fish chowder puree

1 teaspoon olive oil

1 tablespoon finely chopped rindless bacon

¼ trimmed stalk celery (25g), chopped coarsely

½ cup (125ml) hot milk

1 baby new potato (40g), chopped finely

50g firm white fish fillet, chopped coarsely

3 coarsely chopped fresh chives

1 Heat oil in small saucepan; cook bacon and celery,
stirring, until celery softens. Add milk and potato; bring to
the boil. Simmer, uncovered, stirring occasionally, about
8 minutes or until potato is tender. Add fish; simmer,
uncovered, about 2 minutes or until cooked through.

2 Blend or process fish mixture and chives until smooth.
Push through sieve into small bowl.

prep + cook time 25 minutes **makes** ½ cup

nutritional count per tablespoon 4.5g total fat
(1.2g saturated fat); 255kJ (61 cal); 1.8g carbohydrate;
3.2g protein; 0.2g fibre

tip Not suitable to freeze.

carrot and broccolini puree

2 medium carrots (240g), chopped coarsely

125g broccolini, chopped coarsely

1 tablespoon water

1 Steam vegetables until tender; drain.

2 Push vegetables through sieve into small bowl;
stir in the water.

prep + cook time 20 minutes **makes** 1 cup

nutritional count per tablespoon 0g total fat
(0g saturated fat); 33kJ (8 cal); 0.9g carbohydrate;
0.6g protein; 0.9g fibre

banana and rockmelon puree

2 tablespoons passionfruit pulp
100g piece ripe rockmelon, chopped coarsely
½ medium ripe banana (100g), chopped coarsely

1 Push passionfruit through sieve over small bowl;
discard seeds.
2 Blend or process remaining ingredients with
passionfruit juice until smooth.

prep time 10 minutes **makes** ⅔ cup
nutritional count per tablespoon 0g total fat
(0g saturated fat); 59kJ (14 cal); 2.7g carbohydrate;
0.3g protein; 0.7g fibre
tips You need 2 passionfruit for this recipe.
This puree is not suitable to freeze.

apple and blueberry puree

2 large red apples (400g), peeled,
  cored, chopped coarsely
½ cup (75g) frozen blueberries
1 tablespoon water

1 Combine ingredients in small saucepan; bring
to the boil. Reduce heat; simmer, covered, about
10 minutes or until fruit is tender.
2 Blend or process mixture until smooth. Push
through sieve into small bowl.

prep + cook time 20 minutes **makes** 1 cup
nutritional count per tablespoon 0g total fat
(0g saturated fat); 75kJ (18 cal); 3.9g carbohydrate;
0.1g protein; 0.6g fibre
tip We used red apples in this recipe because
green apples are often too tart for infants.

pear and date puree

2 medium pears (460g), peeled, chopped coarsely
3 fresh dates (60g), seeded, chopped coarsely
¼ cup (60ml) water

1 Combine ingredients in small saucepan; bring
to the boil. Reduce heat; simmer, covered, about
10 minutes or until fruit is tender.
2 Blend or process mixture until smooth. Push
through sieve into small bowl.

prep + cook time 20 minutes **makes** 1 cup
nutritional count per tablespoon 0g total fat
(0g saturated fat); 96kJ (23 cal); 5.2g carbohydrate;
0.1g protein; 0.7g fibre

peach and raspberry puree

2 medium ripe peaches (300g), halved
¼ cup (60ml) water
125g fresh or frozen raspberries

1 Preheat oven to 180°C/160°C fan-forced.
2 Place peaches, cut-side down, in ovenproof dish;
add the water. Roast about 15 minutes or until peaches
are tender; cool. Discard skin.
3 Blend or process peaches and raspberries until
smooth. Push through sieve into small bowl.

prep + cook time 25 minutes (+ cooling) **makes** 1 cup
nutritional count per tablespoon 0g total fat
(0g saturated fat); 46kJ (11 cal); 1.9g carbohydrate;
0.3g protein; 0.8g fibre
tip Use ripe peaches as under-ripe fruit will give a
sour tasting puree.

banana and rockmelon puree

apple and blueberry puree

pear and date puree

peach and raspberry puree

eating with the family

Each of these recipes serves 4, with a small amount taken out for your toddler. Cut food into small pieces, if necessary, and make sure it has cooled before serving.

chicken and vegetable risotto

3 cups (750ml) chicken stock

2 cups (500ml) water

1 tablespoon olive oil

300g chicken breast fillets, chopped coarsely

1 medium brown onion (150g), chopped finely

1 clove garlic, crushed

1½ cups (300g) arborio rice

1 cup (120g) frozen peas

2 teaspoons finely grated lemon rind

2 tablespoons finely chopped fresh mint

170g asparagus, trimmed, chopped coarsely

1 Combine stock and the water in medium saucepan; bring to the boil. Reduce heat; simmer, covered.

2 Meanwhile, heat half the oil in large saucepan; cook chicken, in batches, until browned.

3 Heat remaining oil in same pan; cook onion and garlic, stirring, until onion softens. Add rice; stir to coat rice in onion mixture. Add 1 cup simmering stock mixture; cook, stirring, over low heat, until stock is absorbed. Continue adding stock mixture in 1 cup batches, stirring until absorbed between additions. Total cooking time should be about 25 minutes or until rice is tender.

4 Add peas and rind to pan; stir until hot. Remove some risotto for toddler; serve sprinkled with some mint.

5 Add chicken and asparagus to remaining risotto, season to taste; stir until chicken is hot and asparagus is tender. Serve sprinkled with mint.

prep + cook time 55 minutes serves 4

nutritional count per adult serving 10g total fat (2.4g saturated fat); 1944kJ (465 cal); 65g carbohydrate; 26.2g protein; 3.6g fibre

tip Risotto is at its best eaten straight after cooking; it's not suitable to freeze.

potato and bacon frittata

You will need a small ovenproof frying pan
with an 18cm base for this recipe.

1 medium potato (200g), chopped coarsely

6 eggs

½ cup (125ml) milk

¼ cup (20g) finely grated parmesan cheese

1 tablespoon finely chopped fresh flat-leaf parsley

2 rindless bacon rashers (130g), chopped coarsely

3 cherry tomatoes, quartered

20g baby rocket leaves

aïoli

⅓ cup (100g) mayonnaise

2 tablespoons buttermilk

1 clove garlic, crushed

1 Make aïoli.

2 Boil, steam or microwave potato until tender; drain.

3 Combine eggs, milk, cheese and parsley in large jug.

4 Cook bacon in heated oiled medium ovenproof frying
pan until browned; drain on absorbent paper. Return
bacon to same pan with potato; pour egg mixture into
pan. Cook over medium heat about 5 minutes or until
frittata is browned underneath and almost set.

5 Meanwhile, preheat grill.

6 Grill frittata about 5 minutes or until browned lightly.

7 Cut a small slice from frittata for toddler; serve with
cherry tomatoes.

8 Serve remaining frittata with rocket leaves and aïoli.

aïoli Whisk ingredients in small bowl until smooth.

prep + cook time 35 minutes **serves** 4

nutritional count per adult serving 23.3g total fat
(6.8g saturated fat); 1450kJ (347 cal); 13.2g carbohydrate;
21g protein; 1.3g fibre

honey and balsamic glazed lamb shanks

8 french-trimmed lamb shanks (1.7kg)
2 cups (500ml) chicken stock
¼ cup (60ml) balsamic vinegar
¼ cup (90g) honey
2 cloves garlic, crushed
400g baby new potatoes
400g pumpkin, chopped coarsely
2 teaspoons olive oil
150g green beans, trimmed

1 Preheat oven to 220°C/200°C fan-forced.
2 Combine lamb, stock, vinegar, honey and garlic in large flameproof dish. Bring to the boil over high heat; remove from heat, cover tightly.
3 Transfer dish to oven; cook shanks, turning once, about 2 hours or until lamb is tender.
4 Meanwhile, combine potato and pumpkin in small shallow baking dish; drizzle with oil. Roast, uncovered, with lamb, about 45 minutes.
5 Boil, steam or microwave beans until tender; drain.
6 For toddler, mash a little potato and pumpkin in a small bowl until almost smooth. Remove some meat from a lamb shank, chop coarsely; serve with vegetable mash.
7 Season remaining lamb and vegetables to taste before serving.

prep + cook time 2 hours 20 minutes **serves** 4
nutritional count per adult serving 7.4g total fat (2.7g saturated fat); 1935kJ (463 cal); 38.8g carbohydrate; 57.3g protein; 4.3g fibre
tips Remove skin from cooked potato if necessary. Honey may contain harmful bacteria and is not recommended for children under one year old.

honeyed chicken drumsticks

8 chicken drumsticks (1kg)
1 tablespoon honey
¼ cup (60ml) japanese soy sauce
1 teaspoon ground cinnamon
1 tablespoon peanut oil
2 cloves garlic, crushed
2 tablespoons sweet chilli sauce
2 teaspoons finely chopped fresh coriander root and stem mixture
3cm piece fresh ginger (15g), grated
1 tablespoon dry sherry
1 teaspoon sesame seeds
1 cup (200g) jasmine rice

1 Slash chicken several times through thickest parts of drumsticks.
2 Combine honey, soy, cinnamon, oil and garlic in large bowl. Combine 2 tablespoons of the honey mixture with one drumstick in a small bowl for the toddler. Cover; refrigerate 3 hours or overnight.
3 Add remaining chicken, sweet chilli sauce, coriander, ginger and sherry to large bowl. Refrigerate overnight.
4 Preheat oven to 220°C/200°C fan-forced.
5 Place all chicken on oiled wire rack over large baking dish; pour excess marinades over chicken, sprinkle with seeds. Cook, uncovered, about 35 minutes.
6 Boil, steam or microwave rice until tender.
7 Chop flesh from toddler's drumstick; serve with rice.
8 Season remaining chicken and rice to taste.

prep + cook time 45 minutes (+ refrigeration) **serves** 4
nutritional count per adult serving 23g total fat (6.3g saturated fat); 2249kJ (538 cal); 48.2g carbohydrate; 32.4g protein; 1.3g fibre
note Honey may contain harmful bacteria and is not recommended for children under one year old.

tips The cooked lamb can be removed from the bones, and the meat frozen for 2 months. Thaw in the fridge overnight. Vegetables need to be roasted, then served.

honey and balsamic glazed lamb shanks

honeyed chicken drumsticks

tips Sprinkle finely chopped fresh coriander leaves over the chicken to serve. The chicken marinade mixture can be frozen for 2 months; thaw in the fridge overnight.

tips Soak the bamboo skewers in water for at least one hour before using to prevent scorching. The chicken can be marinaded overnight, then skewered and cooked close to serving. The marinaded chicken mixture can be frozen for up to 2 months; thaw overnight in the fridge. Couscous is best made just before serving.

oregano chicken kebabs
with herb couscous

2 tablespoons finely chopped fresh oregano

2 teaspoons finely grated lemon rind

1 tablespoon lemon juice

2 cloves garlic, crushed

500g chicken tenderloins, chopped coarsely

1 teaspoon ground coriander

½ teaspoon ground cumin

½ teaspoon dried chilli flakes

½ cup (140g) yogurt

herb couscous

²/₃ cup (160ml) chicken stock

¾ cup (150g) couscous

2 tablespoons lemon juice

¼ cup finely chopped fresh flat-leaf parsley

1 Combine oregano, rind, juice and garlic in small bowl. Combine a sprinkling of the oregano mixture with a few pieces of the chicken in a small bowl for the toddler; cover, refrigerate 1 hour.

2 Combine remaining oregano mixture, remaining chicken, spices and chilli in medium bowl; cover, refrigerate 1 hour.

3 Thread chicken for toddler onto one bamboo skewer. Thread remaining chicken onto eight bamboo skewers. Cook skewers on heated oiled grill plate (or grill or barbecue) until cooked.

4 Meanwhile, make herb couscous.

5 Remove chicken for toddler from skewer. Serve chicken with a little of the herb couscous.

6 Season remaining chicken and herb couscous to taste; serve with yogurt.

herb couscous Bring stock to the boil in small saucepan; remove from heat, add couscous and juice. Cover couscous; stand 5 minutes, fluffing with fork occasionally. Stir in parsley.

prep + cook time 40 minutes (+ refrigeration) **serves** 4

nutritional count per adult serving 8.5g total fat (3g saturated fat); 1430kJ (342 cal); 31.3g carbohydrate; 34g protein; 1g fibre

creamy chicken crêpes

1 tablespoon finely chopped fresh chervil
2 green onions, chopped finely
50g butter
150g button mushrooms, sliced thinly
2 cloves garlic, crushed
¼ cup (60ml) dry white wine
¼ cup (35g) plain flour
3 cups (750ml) hot milk
2 cups (320g) shredded cooked chicken
crêpe batter
¾ cup (110g) plain flour
1½ cups (375ml) milk
1 egg

1 Make crêpe batter.
2 Heat oiled 24cm heavy-based frying pan; pour
2 tablespoons batter into pan. Cook over low heat until
browned. Turn crêpe; brown other side, remove from pan.
3 Stir chervil and half the onion into remaining batter.
Pour ¼ cup batter into pan, cook until browned; turn crêpe,
brown other side. Remove crêpe from pan. Repeat with
remaining batter to make eight crêpes.
4 Melt 20g of the butter in same pan; cook mushrooms
and garlic. Add wine; boil until liquid has evaporated.
5 Meanwhile, melt remaining butter in medium saucepan.
Add flour; cook, stirring, until mixture bubbles and thickens.
Gradually add milk; cook, stirring, until mixture boils and
thickens. Add chicken and remaining onion; stir until hot.
6 Remove chicken mixture for toddler; use to fill crêpe.
7 Stir mushroom mixture into remaining chicken mixture,
season to taste; use to fill crêpes.
crêpe batter Whisk ingredients in medium bowl until
smooth; strain mixture into large jug, stand 30 minutes.
prep + cook time 1 hour (+ standing) **serves** 4
nutritional count per adult serving 27.9g total fat
(15.8g saturated fat); 2399kJ (574 cal); 40.5g carbohydrate;
36.2g protein; 2.7g fibre

pork and vegetable sang choy bow

1 tablespoon peanut oil
1 small carrot (70g), chopped finely
115g baby corn, chopped finely
1 stalk celery (150g), trimmed, chopped finely
2cm piece fresh ginger (10g), grated
2 cloves garlic, crushed
700g pork mince
¼ cup (60ml) beef stock
1 baby cos lettuce, leaves separated
1 tablespoon kecap manis
2 teaspoons sambal oelek
2 tablespoons lime juice
½ cup (40g) bean sprouts
¼ cup loosely packed fresh coriander leaves

1 Heat oil in wok; stir-fry carrot, corn, celery, ginger and
garlic until vegetables are tender. Add mince; stir-fry until
mince browns. Add stock; bring to the boil.
2 Remove of little of the pork mixture for toddler; serve
with some finely shredded lettuce.
3 Add kecap manis, sambal oelek, juice and sprouts to
wok, season to taste; stir-fry until hot.
4 Divide pork mixture onto remaining lettuce leaves;
serve sprinkled with coriander.
prep + cook time 35 minutes **serves** 4
nutritional count per adult serving 17.5g total fat
(5.4g saturated fat); 1463kJ (350 cal); 8g carbohydrate;
38.2g protein; 3.9g fibre

creamy chicken crêpes

tips Serve with salad for the family and cherry tomatoes for the toddler. We used the meat from half a barbecued chicken in this recipe. Crêpes can be made and frozen, layered with freezer-friendly plastic wrap, for 2 months. Thaw crêpes in the fridge overnight. Warm crêpes, wrapped in foil, in a slow oven for about 10 minutes. Chicken filling (without mushroom mixture) can be made a day ahead; keep covered in the fridge. Reheat filling in the microwave oven, or in a saucepan over a low heat, before adding the mushroom mixture.

tip The mince filling can be made several hours ahead; keep covered in the fridge. Stir-fry over a medium heat to reheat.

pork and vegetable sang choy bow

banana, malt and honey smoothie

Blend or process ⅓ cup milk, ½ small coarsely chopped ripe banana,
1 teaspoon malted milk powder and ½ teaspoon honey until smooth.

prep time 2 minutes **makes** ½ cup (125ml)

nutritional count per ½ cup 3.5g total fat (2.2g saturated fat); 497kJ
(119 cal); 17.5g carbohydrate; 3.9g protein; 1g fibre

note Honey may contain harmful bacteria and is not recommended
for children under one year old.

mango smoothie

Blend or process ⅓ cup milk and ¼ small coarsely chopped ripe mango
until smooth.

prep time 2 minutes **makes** ½ cup (125ml)

nutritional count per ½ cup 3.3g total fat (2.1g saturated fat); 368kJ
(88 cal); 10.7g carbohydrate; 3.3g protein; 0.8g fibre

mixed berry yogurt smoothie

Blend or process ¼ cup milk, ¼ cup fresh or frozen mixed berries and
1 tablespoon yogurt until smooth; strain before serving.

prep time 5 minutes **makes** ½ cup (125ml)

nutritional count per ½ cup 3.2g total fat (2.1g saturated fat); 276kJ
(66 cal); 5.2g carbohydrate; 3.7g protein; 0.9g fibre

peach and apricot smoothie

Blend or process ⅓ cup milk, ½ small coarsely chopped ripe peach and
½ coarsely chopped ripe apricot until smooth; strain before serving.

prep time 5 minutes **makes** ½ cup (125ml)

nutritional count per ½ cup 3.3g total fat (2.1g saturated fat); 334kJ
(80 cal); 8.5g carbohydrate; 3.4g protein; 1.1g fibre

strawberry and soy smoothie

Blend or process ⅓ cup soy milk and 4 fresh or frozen strawberries
until smooth; strain before serving.

prep time 5 minutes **makes** ½ cup (125ml)

nutritional count per ½ cup 1.9g total fat (0.3g saturated fat); 188kJ
(45 cal); 3.5g carbohydrate; 3g protein; 1.5g fibre

Milo and banana smoothie

Blend or process ½ small coarsely chopped ripe banana, ¼ cup milk,
2 teaspoons Milo and 1 tablespoon vanilla ice-cream until smooth.

prep time 2 minutes **makes** ½ cup (125ml)

nutritional count per ½ cup 4.1g total fat (2.6g saturated fat); 581kJ
(139 cal); 20.7g carbohydrate; 4.1g protein; 1.5g fibre

mixed berry
yogurt smoothie

smoothies

The quantities will be too much for your baby to start with, so give her a little, and freeze the rest in an ice-block container for later.

mango smoothie

peach and apricot smoothie

strawberry and soy smoothie

Milo and banana smoothie

banana, malt and honey smoothie

tips Use the rest of the cabbage for another meal; it will keep in the fridge for about 2 days. Cabbage rolls are best made just before serving.

pork cabbage rolls

meatballs napolitana

tips Some butchers sell pork and veal mince as one mince, others sell pork and veal mince separately; they all work well for this recipe. The meatball and sauce recipe can be made ahead and frozen for up to 2 months. Thaw in the fridge overnight. Reheat gently in a saucepan or a microwave oven. Garlic parmesan toasts are best made close to serving.

pork cabbage rolls

1 small savoy cabbage (1.2kg)

400g pork mince

¾ cup (115g) cooked white long-grain rice

¼ cup (40g) dried currants

1 medium tomato (150g), seeded, chopped finely

1 clove garlic, crushed

1 cup (250ml) chicken stock

400g can diced tomatoes

2 sprigs fresh thyme

1 Preheat oven to 200°C/180°C fan-forced.

2 Remove eight leaves from cabbage. Drop leaves, one or two at a time, into large saucepan of boiling water. Boil leaves about 1 minute or until soft and pliable; drain. Trim and discard hard ribs from each leaf; pat leaves dry with absorbent paper.

3 Combine mince, rice, currants, tomato and garlic in medium bowl.

4 Place ¼ cup mince mixture in centre of each cabbage leaf; fold in sides, roll to enclose filling.

5 Place rolls, seam-side down, in single layer, in medium baking dish. Combine stock, undrained tomatoes and thyme in large jug; pour over rolls. Cook, covered, about 40 minutes or until rolls are cooked through. Discard thyme.

6 Serve toddler some cabbage roll with a little sauce.

7 Season remaining sauce to taste; serve with remaining pork and cabbage rolls.

prep + cook time 1 hour 30 minutes **serves** 4

nutritional count per adult serving 7.9g total fat (2.7g saturated fat); 1308kJ (313 cal); 25.8g carbohydrate; 28g protein; 12.8g fibre

meatballs napolitana

500g pork and veal mince

1 egg

½ cup (50g) packaged breadcrumbs

¼ cup (20g) finely grated parmesan cheese

¼ cup finely chopped fresh flat-leaf parsley

1 tablespoon olive oil

1 small brown onion (80g), chopped finely

1 clove garlic, crushed

700g bottled tomato pasta sauce

½ cup (60g) frozen peas

¼ cup coarsely chopped fresh basil

½ cup (60g) seeded green olives

¼ teaspoon dried chilli flakes

garlic parmesan toasts

1 small french bread stick (150g), sliced thickly

1 clove garlic, halved

⅓ cup (25g) finely grated parmesan cheese

1 Combine mince, egg, crumbs, cheese and parsley in medium bowl. Roll level tablespoons of mixture into balls.

2 Heat half the oil in large frying pan; cook meatballs, remove from pan. Heat remaining oil in same pan; cook onion and garlic. Add sauce; bring to the boil. Add meatballs; simmer, uncovered, until sauce thickens slightly.

3 Meanwhile, make garlic parmesan toasts.

4 Add peas and basil to meatballs; simmer 5 minutes.

5 Serve toddler some meatball mixture with toast.

6 Add olives and chilli to remaining meatball mixture; serve with remaining toasts.

garlic parmesan toasts Preheat grill. Toast bread slices one side; rub with garlic. Sprinkle untoasted side with cheese; grill until melted.

prep + cook time 1 hour **serves** 4

nutritional count per adult serving 21.7g total fat (7.2g saturated fat); 2408kJ (576 cal); 50.4g carbohydrate; 41g protein; 6.9g fibre

potato smash with beef and eggplant

500g baby new potatoes

1 tablespoon olive oil

1 medium eggplant (300g), peeled, chopped coarsely

2 cups (500g) bolognese sauce (see page 45)

½ cup (125ml) water

1 tablespoon finely chopped fresh flat-leaf parsley

½ teaspoon dried chilli flakes

1 Preheat oven to 220°C/200°C fan-forced.

2 Place potatoes in small shallow baking dish; drizzle with half the oil. Roast about 40 minutes or until tender. Press potatoes with back of a fork or potato masher until skins burst.

3 Meanwhile, heat remaining oil in large saucepan; cook eggplant, stirring, until browned and tender. Remove from pan.

4 Combine bolognese sauce and the water in same pan; cook, stirring until heated through. Serve toddler some of the bolognese with a little crushed potato; sprinkle with a little of the parsley.

5 Add eggplant and chilli to remaining bolognese sauce, season to taste; cook, stirring, until heated through. Serve bolognese mixture with remaining potato; sprinkle with remaining parsley.

prep + cook time 1 hour **serves** 4

nutritional count per adult serving 8.7 g total fat (1.9g saturated fat); 1212kJ (290 cal); 36.1g carbohydrate; 13.4g protein; 6.2g fibre

tip This recipe is
best made close
to serving.

ratatouille pasta salad

375g rigatoni pasta

½ rindless bacon rasher (30g), chopped coarsely

1 chorizo sausage (170g), sliced thinly

2 cups (400g) reserved ratatouille (see page 50)

⅓ cup (25g) shaved parmesan cheese

⅓ cup (50g) semi-dried tomatoes in oil, drained, chopped coarsely

¼ cup firmly packed fresh small basil leaves

1 Cook pasta in large saucepan of boiling water until tender. Reserve ¼ cup of the cooking liquid; drain pasta. Coarsely chop a little of the cooked pasta for toddler.

2 Meanwhile, cook bacon and chorizo, separately, in medium heated frying pan, stirring, until crisp. Drain separately on absorbent paper.

3 Combine toddler's pasta, all the bacon, 1 tablespoon reserved cooking liquid and some ratatouille in small bowl.

4 Combine remaining pasta, ratatouille and reserved cooking liquid with chorizo, cheese, tomato and basil in large bowl, season to taste; divide into serving bowls.

prep + cook time 25 minutes **serves** 4

nutritional count per adult serving 25.2g total fat (7.6g saturated fat); 2642kJ (632 cal); 72.6g carbohydrate; 25g protein; 6.6g fibre

tuna potato salad

2 medium potatoes (400g), unpeeled, chopped coarsely

100g green beans, trimmed, halved crossways

200g tuna steak

1 tablespoon drained canned tuna in springwater

250g grape tomatoes, halved

80g baby spinach leaves

⅓ cup (40g) seeded black olives

lemon dressing

⅓ cup (80ml) lemon juice

2 tablespoons olive oil

1 clove garlic, crushed

¼ teaspoon ground cumin

1 Boil, steam or microwave potato and beans, separately, until tender; drain. Rinse beans under cold water; drain.

2 Meanwhile, make lemon dressing.

3 Cook tuna steak on heated oiled grill plate (or grill or barbecue) until cooked as desired. Cover tuna, stand 5 minutes; slice thinly.

4 Combine the canned tuna, tomato, spinach, potato, beans and the toddler's dressing in small bowl.

5 Divide remaining ingredients onto serving plates; top with sliced tuna, season to taste; drizzle with remaining lemon dressing.

lemon dressing Combine juice and oil in screw-top jar; shake well. Reserve a little of the dressing for toddler's salad. Add garlic and cumin to remaining dressing, season to taste; shake until combined.

prep + cook time 30 minutes **serves** 4

nutritional count per adult serving 12.5g total fat (2.5g saturated fat); 1062kJ (254 cal); 16.1g carbohydrate; 17.4g protein; 3.8g fibre

ratatouille pasta salad

tips You could substitute the bacon and chorizo with ham and mild salami if you prefer. This recipe can be eaten in several different ways – hot, cold, or hot pasta with cold ratatouille, turning it into a warm salad. Pasta is at its best cooked and eaten straight away, however, for small – usually chopped up – portions for toddlers, freeze pasta in small quantities. The same goes for any leftover ratatouille – which make quick, healthy, easy instant meals for toddlers. Both the ratatouille and pasta thaw well in the microwave oven.

tips You need about half a small can of tuna for your toddler; keep the rest in the fridge for up to 2 days. This salad is all about last-minute assembly. Leftover or drained canned potatoes can be used in place of fresh potatoes.

tuna potato salad

chicken and mango casserole

1 medium mango (430g), chopped coarsely

8 skinless chicken thigh cutlets (1.5kg)

¼ cup (35g) plain flour

2 tablespoons olive oil

1 medium brown onion (150g), chopped finely

2 cloves garlic, crushed

1 teaspoon ground coriander

1 teaspoon ground cumin

1 cup (250ml) chicken stock

¾ cup (150g) jasmine rice

1 tablespoon coarsely chopped fresh flat-leaf parsley

1 Preheat oven to 180°C/160°C fan-forced.

2 Blend or process mango until smooth. You should have ¾ cup (180ml) puree.

3 Toss chicken in flour; shake off excess. Heat half the oil in large flameproof dish; cook chicken, in batches, until browned.

4 Add remaining oil to same dish, cook onion, garlic, coriander and cumin, stirring, until onion softens. Add chicken, stock and mango puree; bring to the boil. Cover; transfer to oven, bake 25 minutes. Uncover; bake about 20 minutes or until chicken is cooked through. Cut some of the chicken meat into pieces for toddler. Season remaining mixture to taste.

5 Meanwhile, cook rice following packet instructions.

6 Serve toddler the chicken pieces with some of the rice and a drizzle of the mango sauce.

7 Divide remaining rice, chicken cutlets and mango sauce into serving bowls; sprinkle with parsley.

prep + cook time 1 hour **serves** 4

nutritional count per adult serving 27.5g total fat (6.9g saturated fat); 2717kJ (650 cal); 48.2g carbohydrate; 51.1g protein; 2.6g fibre

tips This recipe is at its best made just before serving. It's always handy to have rice cooked and frozen in user-friendly portions. Thaw and reheat frozen rice in a microwave oven.

tips If you think the bolognese sauce is a little acid-tasting, add a teaspoon or two of sugar. The sauce can be frozen in user-friendly portions; thaw in the fridge over-night or reheat in a microwave oven. Pasta is always at its best eaten "al dente", which is just after it's cooked. Toddlers don't worry too much about "al dente", so freeze any leftover pasta in small portions for your toddler.

spaghetti bolognese

chicken casserole

tips You could use mixed char-grilled vegetables from a delicatessen instead of the bottled variety. This recipe is best made just before serving; it's not suitable to freeze because the mushrooms will become tough and rubbery.

spaghetti bolognese

1 tablespoon olive oil
1 medium brown onion (150g), chopped finely
2 cloves garlic, crushed
1 medium carrot (120g), chopped finely
1 stalk celery (150g), trimmed, chopped finely
500g lean beef mince
2 x 400g cans crushed tomatoes
1/3 cup (95g) tomato paste
2 tablespoons finely chopped fresh basil
375g spaghetti
1/4 cup (20g) finely grated parmesan cheese

1 Heat oil in large saucepan; cook onion, garlic, carrot and celery, stirring, until vegetables soften. Add mince; cook, stirring, about 5 minutes or until mince is browned. Add undrained tomatoes and paste; bring to the boil. Reduce heat; simmer, uncovered, about 15 minutes or until sauce thickens. Add basil; simmer, uncovered, 5 minutes. Reserve 2 cups of mixture for potato smash with bolognese and eggplant recipe (see page 38).
2 Meanwhile, cook pasta in large saucepan boiling water until tender; drain. Reserve a little of the pasta for toddler; chop pasta coarsely.
3 Combine toddler's pasta and some of the bolognese sauce in small bowl.
4 Divide remaining pasta into serving bowls. Season remaining bolognese sauce to taste, spoon over pasta; sprinkle with cheese.
prep + cook time 35 minutes **serves** 4
nutritional count per adult serving 16.4g total fat (5.5g saturated fat); 2671kJ (639 cal); 76.5g carbohydrate; 41.1g protein; 8.5g fibre

chicken casserole

1 tablespoon olive oil
8 chicken drumsticks (1kg)
1 medium brown onion (150g), chopped coarsely
150g button mushrooms, quartered
2 cloves garlic, crushed
2 tablespoons tomato paste
400g can diced tomatoes
1 cup (250ml) chicken stock
2 sprigs fresh thyme
1/3 cup (70g) bottled char-grilled vegetables, drained
cheesy polenta
3 cups (750ml) milk
3/4 cup (125g) polenta
1/4 cup (20g) finely grated parmesan cheese

1 Preheat oven to 180°C/160°C fan-forced.
2 Heat oil in large flameproof dish; brown chicken in batches. Cook onion, mushrooms and garlic in same dish, add paste, undrained tomatoes, stock, thyme and chicken; bring to the boil. Cover; transfer to oven, bake 25 minutes. Uncover; bake 20 minutes. Discard thyme. Shred chicken meat for toddler.
3 Meanwhile, make cheesy polenta.
4 Place polenta into bowl for toddler, top with chicken, then tomato mixture.
5 Coarsely chop char-grilled vegetables; add to remaining tomato mixture. Serve remaining polenta with tomato mixture and remaining chicken.
cheesy polenta Bring milk to the boil in medium saucepan, gradually stir in polenta. Simmer, stirring, about 10 minutes or until polenta thickens. Stir in cheese.
prep + cook time 1 hour **serves** 4
nutritional count per adult serving 34.3g total fat (12.6g saturated fat); 2725kJ (652 cal); 37.9g carbohydrate; 45.6g protein; 4.7g fibre

Vegemite and cheese pinwheels

Preheat oven to 200°C/180°C fan-forced. Oil 19cm x 30cm lamington pan. Sift
2 cups self-raising flour and 1 tablespoon caster sugar into medium bowl; rub in
50g chopped butter. Stir in ¾ cup milk, mix to a soft sticky dough. Turn dough
onto floured surface; knead lightly until smooth. Roll dough to 30cm x 40cm shape.
Spread 2 tablespoons Vegemite over dough; sprinkle with 1¼ cups coarsely grated
cheddar cheese. Starting from long side, roll dough firmly; trim ends. Cut roll into
12 slices; place pinwheels, cut-side up, in single layer, in pan. Bake about 30 minutes.
Serve pinwheels warm.

prep + cook time 40 minutes   **makes** 12

nutritional count per pinwheel 8.5g total fat (5.4g saturated fat); 761kJ
(182 cal); 19g carbohydrate; 6.8g protein; 0.9g fibre

tip Unbaked pinwheels can be frozen for up to a month. Bake them from frozen,
adding about 10 minutes to the baking time.

spinach and cheese monster scones

Preheat oven to 240°C/220°C fan-forced. Oil deep 20cm-square cake pan. Thaw
a 250g packet of finely chopped frozen spinach; squeeze out excess liquid. Sift
2½ cups self-raising flour and 1 tablespoon caster sugar into medium bowl; rub in
50g chopped butter. Stir in ½ cup coarsely grated cheddar cheese and the spinach.
Stir in ¾ cup milk, mix to a soft sticky dough. Turn dough onto floured surface; knead
lightly until smooth. Press dough out to 2cm thickness. Cut 16 x 4.5cm rounds from
dough. Place scones, just touching, in pan. Bake about 20 minutes. Serve warm.

prep + cook time 30 minutes   **makes** 16

nutritional count per scone 4.6g total fat (2.8g saturated fat); 535kJ (128 cal);
17.2g carbohydrate; 3.8g protein; 1.2g fibre

tip Unbaked scones can be frozen for up to a month. Bake them from frozen,
adding about 10 minutes to the baking time.

apple and cinnamon mini muffins

Preheat oven to 180°C/160°C fan-forced. Line two 12-hole (1-tablespoon/20ml)
mini muffin pans with paper cases. Sift ¾ cup self-raising flour and 1 teaspoon
ground cinnamon into medium bowl; stir in $^1/_3$ cup firmly packed brown sugar and
¼ cup rolled oats. Stir in combined ¼ cup milk, ¼ cup apple juice, ¼ cup vegetable
oil and 1 egg. Add ¼ cup coarsely grated, peeled apple; stir gently to combine.
Divide mixture into paper cases. Bake muffins about 15 minutes. Stand 5 minutes
before turning, top-side up, onto wire rack to cool.

prep + cook time 25 minutes   **makes** 24

nutritional count per muffin 2.8g total fat (0.5g saturated fat); 234kJ (56 cal);
6.5g carbohydrate; 0.9g protein; 0.2g fibre

tips Serve dusted with sifted icing sugar, if you like. Store muffins in an airtight
container for up to two days, or freeze for up to one month.

healthy snacks

Kids love snacks – give them small amounts of food often,
but make sure it's healthy most of the time.

spinach and cheese monster scones

apple and cinnamon mini muffins

Vegemite and cheese pinwheels

fruit and cereal snack

Preheat oven to 180°C/160°C fan-forced. Combine ½ cup rice bubbles, ½ cup cornflakes and 1 cup flaked coconut in large shallow baking dish; roast, uncovered, about 5 minutes, stirring occasionally. Transfer to large bowl; cool. Stir in ½ cup finely chopped dried pear, ⅓ cup finely chopped dried apple, ¼ cup finely chopped seeded prunes and ½ cup dried cranberries.

prep + cook time 20 minutes (+ cooling) **makes** 3½ cups

nutritional count per ¼ cup 3.6g total fat (3.1g saturated fat); 322kJ (77 cal); 9.7g carbohydrate; 0.7g protein; 2.1g fibre

tips Store in an airtight container in the refrigerator for up to 1 month. Change the fruit to suit your child's taste. We've allowed ¼ cup of the snack per serve. This fruit and cereal snack is also used in the muesli lunchbox cookies on page 110.

chicken and corn dip

Bring 2 cups water to the boil in small saucepan; add one 200g chicken breast fillet. Reduce heat; simmer, covered, about 10 minutes or until chicken is cooked. Cool chicken in liquid 10 minutes; drain. Shred chicken finely using two forks. Combine chicken, 250g cream cheese, 2 x 125g cans creamed corn, 2 tablespoons finely chopped fresh flat-leaf parsley and 1 tablespoon finely chopped fresh chives in medium bowl.

prep + cook time 20 minutes (+ cooling) **makes** 2½ cups

nutritional count per tablespoon 7.9g total fat (4.7g saturated fat); 460kJ (110 cal); 4g carbohydrate; 5.7g protein; 0.7g fibre

tips Serve dip with toasted torn pitta bread, vegetable sticks or crackers, if you like. Use any leftover dip as a sandwich filling. This recipe is not suitable for freezing.

muesli slice

Preheat oven to 160°C/140°C fan-forced. Grease 24cm x 32cm swiss roll pan; line base with baking paper, extending paper 5cm over long sides. Combine 1½ cups cornflakes, 1½ cups rolled oats, 1 cup rice bubbles, ½ cup shredded coconut and 400g can skim sweetened condensed milk in large bowl; press mixture firmly into pan. Bake about 40 minutes or until browned lightly; cool in pan. Lift slice from pan; cut slice into bars.

prep + cook time 50 minutes (+ cooling) **makes** 24

nutritional count per slice 3.1g total fat (2g saturated fat); 426kJ (102 cal); 15.6g carbohydrate; 2.3g protein; 0.7g fibre

tip The slice will keep in an airtight container for up to a week; slice can also be frozen for up to a month.

muesli slice

fruit and cereal snack

chicken and corn dip

cheesy pumpkin polenta fingers

500g piece pumpkin, chopped coarsely

2 tablespoons olive oil

3 cups (750ml) water

¾ cup (125g) polenta

¼ cup (20g) finely grated parmesan cheese

20g baby rocket leaves

ratatouille

1 small eggplant (230g)

2 medium zucchini (240g)

1 medium red capsicum (200g)

2 tablespoons olive oil

½ small red onion (50g), chopped coarsely

2 cloves garlic, crushed

400g can crushed tomatoes

½ cup (130g) bottled tomato pasta sauce

½ cup (125ml) water

¼ cup loosely packed fresh small basil leaves

1 Preheat oven to 220°C/200°C fan-forced. Grease deep 20cm-square cake pan.

2 Toss pumpkin with half the oil in medium shallow baking dish; roast, in single layer, 30 minutes.

3 Place the water in medium saucepan; bring to the boil. Gradually add polenta to water, stirring constantly, reduce heat. Simmer, stirring, about 10 minutes or until polenta thickens. Remove from heat, stir in cheese and pumpkin; spread into pan, cool 10 minutes. Cover; refrigerate about 1 hour or until firm.

4 Meanwhile, make ratatouille.

5 Turn polenta onto board; trim edges. Cut into quarters; cut each quarter into three slices. Heat remaining oil in large frying pan; cook polenta until browned all over. Reserve a slice of polenta for toddler; cut into bite-sized pieces. Place toddler's polenta on serving plate; top with some of the ratatouille.

6 Divide remaining polenta slices onto serving plates; top with remaining ratatouille, serve with rocket.

ratatouille Peel eggplant; randomly peel zucchini. Chop eggplant, zucchini and capsicum into 1cm pieces. Heat half the oil in large frying pan; cook eggplant and zucchini, stirring, until browned all over. Remove from pan. Heat remaining oil in same pan; cook capsicum, onion and garlic, stirring, until onion softens. Add undrained tomatoes, sauce, the water and eggplant mixture; bring to the boil. Simmer, uncovered, about 10 minutes or until vegetables are tender. Remove from heat; stir in basil. Reserve 2 cups for ratatouille pasta salad recipe (see page 40).

prep + cook time 1 hour 10 minutes (+ refrigeration)

serves 4

nutritional count per adult serving 21.8g total fat (4g saturated fat); 1689kJ (404 cal); 38.5g carbohydrate; 10.2g protein; 7.2g fibre

note Ratatouille can be stored, covered, in the fridge for 3 days, or frozen for 1 month.

tips Add a little sugar to the ratatouille to reduce any acid taste. It's not essential to peel the eggplant or zucchini, but if by peeling them the toddler will eat these vegies, then it's worth the effort. If you want to reduce or eliminate the oil, the ratatouille can be cooked in the oven. Combine all the ingredients in an ovenproof dish and bake at 180°C/160°C fan-forced for about 30 minutes.

lamb and kidney bean cassoulet

400g lamb sausages, sliced thickly

2 rindless bacon rashers (130g), chopped coarsely

1 medium brown onion (150g), chopped coarsely

2 cloves garlic, crushed

1 sprig fresh rosemary

2 bay leaves

400g can crushed tomatoes

420g can kidney beans, rinsed, drained

1 cup (250ml) chicken stock

2 cups (140g) stale breadcrumbs

1/3 cup coarsely chopped fresh flat-leaf parsley

1 Preheat oven to 180°C/160°C fan-forced.

2 Cook sausages in large flameproof dish over medium heat until browned all over; remove from dish. Cook bacon in same dish, stirring, until crisp; remove from dish.

3 Cook onion and garlic in same dish, stirring, until onion softens. Add rosemary, bay leaves, undrained tomatoes, beans, stock, sausages and bacon; bring to the boil. Cover; transfer to oven, bake 30 minutes. Remove from oven, remove rosemary and bay leaves; sprinkle with combined breadcrumbs and parsley. Return to oven; bake, uncovered, about 35 minutes or until liquid is nearly absorbed.

4 Serve about ½ cup cassoulet to toddler.

5 Divide remaining cassoulet into serving bowls; season to taste.

prep + cook time 1 hour 20 minutes **serves** 4

nutritional count per adult serving 24.7g total fat (9.7g saturated fat); 2479kJ (593 cal); 45.3g carbohydrate; 42.9g protein; 8.8g fibre

tips This is a complete meal in a dish, but it doesn't reheat or freeze well as the breadcrumbs absorb the moisture as it stands. Packaged Japanese breadcrumbs (panko) can be bought from Asian food stores that stock Japanese ingredients; they're an excellent substitute for stale breadcrumbs.

lamb stew with buttermilk mash

2 tablespoons olive oil

700g diced lamb

1 medium brown onion (150g), chopped coarsely

1 large carrot (180g), chopped coarsely

2 stalks celery (300g), trimmed, chopped coarsely

2 cups (500ml) beef stock

400g can diced tomatoes

150g button mushrooms, halved

½ cup (60g) frozen peas

½ cup (60g) coarsely grated cheddar cheese

buttermilk mash

4 medium potatoes (800g), chopped coarsely

½ cup (125ml) buttermilk, warmed

1 Heat half the oil in large saucepan; cook lamb, in batches, until browned.

2 Heat remaining oil in same pan; cook onion, stirring, until onion softens. Return lamb to pan with carrot, celery, stock and undrained tomatoes. Bring to the boil. Reduce heat; simmer, covered, 1 hour. Uncover; simmer 30 minutes.

3 Add mushrooms; simmer, uncovered, about 30 minutes or until lamb is tender. Add peas; stir until heated through.

4 Meanwhile, make buttermilk mash.

5 Serve toddler some of the lamb mixture over a little of the buttermilk mash.

6 Preheat grill.

7 Divide remaining lamb mixture into four deep 1½-cup (375ml) ovenproof dishes, season to taste; top with mash, sprinkle with cheese. Grill pies until browned lightly.

buttermilk mash Boil, steam or microwave potato until tender; drain. Mash potato with buttermilk in medium bowl until smooth.

prep + cook time 2 hours 30 minutes **serves** 4

nutritional count per adult serving 31.1g total fat (12.1g saturated fat); 2663kJ (637 cal); 33.6g carbohydrate; 51.5g protein; 8.3g fibre

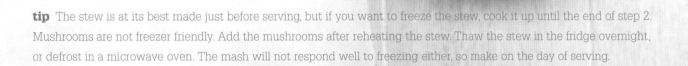

tip The stew is at its best made just before serving, but if you want to freeze the stew, cook it up until the end of step 2. Mushrooms are not freezer friendly. Add the mushrooms after reheating the stew. Thaw the stew in the fridge overnight, or defrost in a microwave oven. The mash will not respond well to freezing either, so make on the day of serving.

27/08/13
This was nice.
Ensure you measure veggies so there's not too many 2
Decrease for 500g of beef.

glazed meatloaf

1 trimmed corn cob (250g)

1 medium carrot (120g), grated coarsely

1 medium zucchini (120g), grated coarsely

1 baby beetroot (25g), peeled, grated coarsely

600g beef mince

1 egg

½ cup (50g) packaged breadcrumbs

2 tablespoons tomato sauce

2 tablespoons barbecue sauce

1 Preheat oven to 200°C/180°C fan-forced. Grease 12cm x 22cm loaf pan.

2 Remove kernels from corn; combine corn, carrot, zucchini, beetroot, mince, egg and breadcrumbs in large bowl. Press mixture into pan.

3 Cover pan with foil; bake 40 minutes. Remove loaf from oven; drain excess juices from pan.

4 Turn pan upside-down onto foil or baking-paper-lined oven tray; remove pan. Brush loaf with combined sauces; bake, uncovered, brushing occasionally with sauce mixture, about 20 minutes or until loaf is cooked through. Stand 10 minutes before slicing thickly.

5 Cut a slice of the meatloaf into fingers for toddler; serve with extra tomato sauce, if you like.

6 Season remaining meatloaf to taste; serve with mustard, horseradish or chutney, if you like.

prep + cook time 1 hour 15 minutes **serves** 4

nutritional count per adult serving 16.3g total fat (6.5g saturated fat); 1655kJ (396 cal); 25.9g carbohydrate; 34g protein; 4.3g fibre

tip Meatloaf is good served hot, warm or cold – serve it as a meal with mash and green vegies or a salad. Cold meatloaf makes a great sandwich filling. Meatloaf doesn't freeze well.

minestrone with cheese toasties

tips The soup is at its best made just before serving as the pasta will keep absorbing liquid from the soup, changing the consistency to a thicker soup. The green beans will also change in colour as the soup stands.

tips Add some thinly sliced red chilli for a spicy version of this soup, if you like. This is a last minute soup; it doesn't freeze well. The pasta will become soggy as it absorbs more liquid and the buk choy will discolour.

chicken, corn and pasta soup

minestrone with cheese toasties

2 teaspoons olive oil

1 small brown onion (80g), chopped finely

1 clove garlic, crushed

1 medium carrot (120g), chopped finely

1 stalk celery (150g), trimmed, chopped finely

1 tablespoon tomato paste

700g bottled tomato pasta sauce

2 cups (500ml) beef stock

2 cups (500ml) water

80g green beans, trimmed, chopped finely

½ cup (65g) small pasta shells

420g can borlotti beans, rinsed, drained

2 tablespoons finely chopped fresh flat-leaf parsley

cheese toasties

5 slices white bread (180g)

¹/₃ cup (35g) coarsely grated mozzarella cheese

1 Heat oil in large saucepan; cook onion, garlic, carrot and celery until vegetables soften. Stir in paste.

2 Add sauce, stock and the water; bring to the boil. Reduce heat; simmer, uncovered, 10 minutes. Add green beans, pasta and borlotti beans; simmer, uncovered, about 15 minutes or until pasta is tender.

3 Meanwhile, make cheese toasties.

4 Sprinkle parsley over toddler's soup; serve with toasties.

5 Season remaining soup, add parsley; serve with toasties.

cheese toasties Preheat grill. Cut two 6cm elephants from one slice of bread. Toast one side of breads; turn, sprinkle with cheese, grill until melted. (Cut adult's toasts into small triangles.)

prep + cook time 1 hour **serves** 4

nutritional count per adult serving 7.6g total fat (2.1g saturated fat); 1710kJ (409 cal); 61.1g carbohydrate; 17.6g protein; 11.8g fibre

chicken, corn and pasta soup

2 teaspoons vegetable oil

2 green onions, sliced thinly

3cm piece fresh ginger (15g), grated

2 cloves garlic, crushed

3 cups (750ml) water

2 cups (500ml) chicken stock

300g chicken breast fillet

420g can creamed corn

½ cup (110g) risoni pasta

1 tablespoon japanese soy sauce

1 baby buk choy (150g), shredded finely

1 Heat oil in large saucepan; cook onion, ginger and garlic, stirring, until onion softens. Add the water and stock; bring to the boil. Add chicken; reduce heat. Simmer, covered, about 10 minutes or until chicken is cooked. Remove from heat; cool chicken in broth 10 minutes. Remove chicken from broth; chop meat finely.

2 Return broth to the boil. Add corn and pasta to pan; simmer, uncovered, about 10 minutes or until pasta is tender. Return chicken to pan; simmer, uncovered, until heated through.

3 Remove some of the soup for toddler to a small bowl.

4 Add sauce and buk choy to remaining soup, season to taste; simmer, uncovered, until buk choy wilts.

prep + cook time 50 minutes **serves** 4

nutritional count per adult serving 8.1g total fat (2g saturated fat); 1388kJ (332 cal); 38.2g carbohydrate; 23.5g protein; 5.4g fibre

spiced moroccan fish with couscous

1 cup (200g) couscous

1 cup (250ml) boiling water

20g butter, chopped coarsely

$2/3$ cup (50g) flaked almonds, roasted

2 tablespoons dried currants

$1/3$ cup coarsely chopped fresh mint

600g white fish fillet

3 teaspoons moroccan seasoning

lemon dressing

2 tablespoons olive oil

2 tablespoons lemon juice

2 teaspoons finely grated lemon rind

2 teaspoons finely chopped preserved lemon

1 Combine couscous with the water in medium heatproof bowl, cover; stand 5 minutes or until liquid is absorbed, fluffing with fork occasionally. Stir in butter. Stand 10 minutes. Stir in nuts and currants; reserve some of the couscous mixture for toddler. Add mint to remaining couscous mixture; season to taste.

2 Meanwhile, make lemon dressing.

3 Cut fish into four large fillets for adults and a smaller fillet for toddler. Rub seasoning all over fish. Cook fish in heated oiled large frying pan.

4 Place toddler's couscous on serving plate. Flake toddler's fish over couscous; drizzle with toddler's lemon dressing.

5 Divide remaining couscous onto serving plates; top with remaining fish fillets and lemon dressing.

lemon dressing Combine oil and juice in screw-top jar; shake well. Reserve a little of the dressing for toddler. Add rind and preserved lemon to remaining dressing; shake well.

prep + cook time 30 minutes (+ standing) serves 4
nutritional count per adult serving 23.9g total fat (5.5g saturated fat); 2316kJ (554 cal); 43.3g carbohydrate; 40g protein; 2.4g fibre

tips Serve the fish dolloped with yogurt. We used blue-eye fillets in this recipe, but any white fish fillet will be fine. We used a mild moroccan seasoning, if you're in doubt about using this for your toddler, don't rub it onto the toddler's fish. Moroccan seasoning is available in the dried herbs and spices section of most supermarkets. You might want to leave the nuts out of the couscous or you might want to chop them – depending on the age of your toddler. This is a last minute recipe and is not suitable to freeze or microwave.

banana and honey fruit loaf sandwich

Spread one slice of fruit loaf with ½ teaspoon honey; top with ½ small thinly
sliced ripe banana and a second slice of fruit loaf. Remove and discard crusts;
cut sandwich into fingers.

prep time 5 minutes **makes** 1

nutritional count per sandwich 2.3g total fat (0.4g saturated fat); 957kJ (229 cal);
44.4g carbohydrate; 5.4g protein; 3.6g fibre

note Honey may contain harmful bacteria and is not recommended for children
under one year old.

peanut butter and alfalfa sandwich

Spread two slices of wholemeal bread with 1 tablespoon smooth peanut butter; top
one slice with ¼ cup alfalfa sprouts and 1 teaspoon sunflower seed kernels. Top
with remaining bread. Remove and discard crusts; cut sandwich into triangles.

prep time 5 minutes **makes** 1

nutritional count per sandwich 15.9g total fat (2.5g saturated fat); 1195kJ
(286 cal); 44.4g carbohydrate; 5.4g protein; 3.6g fibre

note Peanuts can cause allergic reactions in some children; they are not
recommended for children under one year old.

carrot, sultana and cottage cheese sandwich

Combine ½ small coarsely grated carrot, 1 tablespoon cottage cheese and
2 teaspoons sultanas in small bowl. Spread one slice of white bread with
cheese mixture; top with a second slice of white bread. Remove and discard
crusts; cut sandwich into fingers.

prep time 5 minutes **makes** 1

nutritional count per sandwich 2.5g total fat (1g saturated fat); 823kJ (197 cal);
33.6g carbohydrate; 8g protein; 2.7g fibre

sandwiches

Make sure the sandwiches are robust enough to tolerate excessive handling; evenly spread, moist fillings work best for kids.

banana and honey fruit loaf sandwich

carrot, sultana and cottage cheese sandwich

peanut butter and alfalfa sandwich

tuna and baby spinach sandwich

Combine ¼ cup coarsely chopped baby spinach leaves, 1 tablespoon mayonnaise, and ¼ small finely chopped tomato in small bowl. Spread one slice of white bread with half the spinach mixture; top with 3 drained tuna slices in springwater, remaining spinach mixture and a second slice of white bread. Cut sandwich into fish shapes using large fish cutter.

prep time 5 minutes **makes** 1

nutritional count per sandwich 9.4g total fat (1.7g saturated fat); 1246kJ (298 cal); 31g carbohydrate; 20.6g protein; 2.2g fibre

tips For children under one year old, peel and remove seeds from tomato before chopping. We used tuna slices from a 95g can tuna slices in springwater.

chicken and celery sandwich

Combine ¼ cup finely shredded cooked chicken, ½ trimmed finely chopped celery stick, 1 tablespoon mayonnaise, 2 teaspoons finely chopped fresh chives and 1 teaspoon lemon juice in small bowl. Spread one slice of wholemeal bread with chicken mixture; top with a second slice of wholemeal bread. Remove and discard crusts; cut sandwich into fingers.

prep time 10 minutes **makes** 1

nutritional count per sandwich 11.8g total fat (2.1g saturated fat); 1078kJ (258 cal); 22.9g carbohydrate; 12.9g protein; 4.1g fibre

Vegemite, cheese and lettuce sandwich

Spread one slice of white bread with ½ teaspoon Vegemite; top with 1 tablespoon coarsely grated cheddar cheese, 1 tablespoon finely shredded iceberg lettuce and a second slice of white bread. Remove and discard crusts; cut sandwich into squares.

prep time 5 minutes **makes** 1

nutritional count per sandwich 4.6g total fat (2.4g saturated fat); 769kJ (184 cal); 26.7g carbohydrate; 7.9g protein; 1.6g fibre

Vegemite, cheese and lettuce sandwich

chicken and celery sandwich

tuna and baby spinach sandwich

tips This is a hearty wintry recipe, similar to a Lebanese recipe known as mejadra (mujaddara). The lentil and rice mixture could be made ahead and frozen. Thaw in the fridge overnight, or reheat in a microwave oven. You might need to add a little more stock or water to bring the stew to the consistency you like. The onions are best cooked just before serving.

lentil and rice stew

chicken, carrot and fetta patties

tips Patties are best made and cooked just before serving as the cooked patties don't freeze well. Uncooked patties minus the cheese can be stacked, layered with freezer-proof plastic wrap, and frozen for 2 months.

lentil and rice stew

1 cup (200g) brown lentils
1.125L (4½ cups) water
½ cup (100g) white long-grain rice
1 teaspoon ground allspice
4 pocket pitta breads (340g)
½ cup coarsely chopped fresh coriander
caramelised onion
1 tablespoon olive oil
2 medium brown onions (300g), sliced thinly
2 teaspoons brown sugar
1 tablespoon balsamic vinegar
⅓ cup (60ml) water

1 Combine lentils and 2½ cups of the water in medium saucepan; bring to the boil. Reduce heat; simmer, covered, about 25 minutes or until tender. Add rice, the remaining water and allspice; bring to the boil. Reduce heat; simmer, covered, stirring occasionally, about 15 minutes or until rice is tender.
2 Meanwhile, make caramelised onion.
3 Serve toddler a little of the lentil mixture with some of the pitta bread.
4 Season remaining lentil mixture to taste; stir in coriander. Serve bowls of stew topped with caramelised onion, and remaining pitta.
caramelised onion Heat oil in large frying pan; cook onion, stirring, until onion softens. Add sugar, vinegar and the water; cook, stirring, about 10 minutes or until onions are caramelised.
prep + cook time 50 minutes serves 4
nutritional count per adult serving 7.7g total fat (1.1g saturated fat); 2261kJ (541 cal); 88.6g carbohydrate; 22.9g protein; 10.9g fibre

chicken, carrot and fetta patties

700g chicken mince
1 egg
½ cup (50g) packaged breadcrumbs
1 small carrot (70g), grated coarsely
2 green onions, chopped finely
¼ cup finely chopped fresh flat-leaf parsley
100g fetta cheese, crumbled
1 tablespoon olive oil

1 Combine mince, egg, breadcrumbs, carrot, onion and parsley in large bowl.
2 Remove about ¼ cup chicken mixture for toddler; shape into two or three patties.
3 Add cheese to remaining chicken mixture, season to taste; mix well. Shape mixture into 16 patties.
4 Heat oil in large frying pan; cook patties until browned and cooked through.
5 Serve toddler's patties with cherry tomatoes and cucumber sticks, and/or tomato sauce, if you like.
6 Remaining patties can be served with a mango or tomato chutney, a mash and a green salad.
prep + cook time 30 minutes serves 4
nutritional count per adult serving 25.8g total fat (9.1g saturated fat); 1659kJ (397 cal); 1.2g carbohydrate; 39.9g protein; 0.7g fibre

ricotta and spinach pasta bake

32 large pasta shells (280g)

500g spinach, trimmed

600g low-fat ricotta cheese

2 tablespoons finely chopped fresh flat-leaf parsley

1 tablespoon finely chopped fresh mint

700g bottled tomato pasta sauce

½ cup (125ml) chicken stock

2 tablespoons finely grated parmesan cheese

1 Cook pasta in large saucepan of boiling water, 3 minutes; drain. Cool 10 minutes.

2 Preheat oven to 180°C/160°C fan-forced.

3 Boil, steam or microwave spinach until wilted; drain. Chop spinach finely; squeeze out excess liquid.

4 Combine spinach in large bowl with ricotta and herbs; spoon mixture into pasta shells.

5 Combine sauce and stock in oiled shallow 2-litre (8-cup) ovenproof dish. Place pasta shells in dish; sprinkle with parmesan. Bake, covered, about 50 minutes or until pasta is tender. Bake, uncovered, 10 minutes or until browned lightly. Remove from oven; stand 10 minutes.

6 Serve toddler two or three pasta shells in a small bowl; drizzle with a little of the sauce.

7 Divide remaining pasta shells and sauce into serving bowls; season to taste.

prep + cook time 1 hour 20 minutes **serves** 4

nutritional count per adult serving 20.3g total fat (11.9g saturated fat); 2370kJ (567 cal); 63.6g carbohydrate; 28.8g protein; 7.3g fibre

tip Serve the bake with a green salad and crusty bread. This recipe can be prepared 3 hours ahead – keep covered in the fridge ready for baking.

vegetable and chickpea fritters

1½ cups (225g) chickpea (besan) flour

1 large zucchini (150g), grated coarsely

1 large brown onion (200g), grated coarsely

1 large carrot (180g), grated coarsely

¾ cup (120g) frozen peas and corn mix

1 clove garlic, crushed

1 teaspoon ground cumin

1 teaspoon garam marsala

½ teaspoon baking powder

1½ tablespoons water

¼ cup coarsely chopped fresh coriander

vegetable oil for shallow frying

¾ cup (210g) yogurt

1 Combine flour, vegetables, garlic, spices, baking powder and the water in medium bowl.

2 Remove some of the vegetable mixture for toddler; shape into three fritters.

3 Mix coriander into remaining vegetable mixture. Shape mixture into 16 fritters.

4 Heat oil in large shallow frying pan. Shallow-fry fritters, in batches, until browned and cooked through. Drain on absorbent paper.

5 Place toddler's fritters, topped with a little of the yogurt in a small bowl.

6 Season remaining fritters to taste; serve with yogurt for dipping.

prep + cook time 25 minutes **serves** 4

nutritional count per adult serving 17.1g total fat (3.1g saturated fat); 1710kJ (409 cal); 43.7g carbohydrate; 17.9g protein; 10.2g fibre

tips A green salad would go well with these fritters. Your hand is the best "implement" for mixing the fritter ingredients together. This is a last minute recipe; it's not suitable to freeze at any stage.

tips Serve with a green salad. Toddlers and grown-ups alike will love this recipe. The fingers can be prepared several hours ahead of baking. They're not suitable to freeze

pizza fingers

430g loaf turkish bread

¼ cup (65g) basil pesto

¹/₃ cup (50g) semi-dried tomatoes in oil, drained, chopped finely

10 cherry bocconcini (150g), sliced thinly

¼ cup (70g) tomato paste

¹/₃ cup (90g) drained pineapple pieces, chopped coarsely

2 rindless bacon rashers (130g), sliced thinly

½ cup (60g) coarsely grated cheddar cheese

2 tablespoons small fresh basil leaves

1 Preheat oven to 180°C/160°C fan-forced.

2 Cut bread into 2cm-wide slices. Place slices flat on baking-paper-lined oven trays; toast about 10 minutes or until crisp.

3 Spread half the slices with pesto; top with semi-dried tomato and bocconcini. Spread remaining bread slices with tomato paste; top with pineapple, bacon and cheddar. Bake about 12 minutes.

4 Place pizza fingers on platter; top with basil leaves.

prep + cook time 30 minutes **makes** 20

nutritional count per pizza finger 5.2g total fat (2.1g saturated fat); 497kJ (119 cal); 11.4g carbohydrate; 5.9g protein; 1.2g fibre

fish fingers with coleslaw

1kg white fish fillets, skin removed, chopped coarsely

2 tablespoons coarsely chopped fresh chives

2 egg whites

1¼ cups (125g) packaged breadcrumbs

2 tablespoons olive oil

coleslaw

1½ cups (120g) finely shredded red cabbage

1 cup (80g) finely shredded savoy cabbage

1 medium carrot (120g), grated coarsely

2 tablespoons coarsely chopped fresh flat-leaf parsley

1 green onion, sliced thinly

2 tablespoons mayonnaise

1 tablespoon sour cream

1 tablespoon white wine vinegar

1 Make coleslaw.

2 Grease 19cm x 30cm lamington pan.

3 Blend or process fish and chives until smooth. Press mixture evenly into pan, turn onto baking-paper-lined tray; cut into eight 19cm slices; cut each slice in half to make 16 fish fingers.

4 Whisk egg whites lightly in medium shallow bowl; place breadcrumbs in another medium shallow bowl. Dip fish fingers into egg whites, then in breadcrumbs to coat. Heat oil in large frying pan; cook fish fingers, in batches, until browned lightly and cooked through. Drain on absorbent paper.

5 Cut part of a fish finger into pieces for toddler; serve with a little of the coleslaw.

6 Divide remaining fish fingers and coleslaw onto serving plates; season to taste.

coleslaw Combine ingredients in large bowl.

prep + cook time 35 minutes **serves** 4

nutritional count per adult serving 21.1g total fat (4.9g saturated fat); 2240kJ (536 cal); 25.6g carbohydrate; 58.6g protein; 4.1g fibre

tips We used ling fillets in this recipe, but any white fish fillets will do. You could serve the fish fingers with lemon wedges and oven-baked potato wedges. Fish fingers can be crumbed, placed on a tray in a single layer, covered, then refrigerated for several hours ahead of cooking. Coleslaw can be made and refrigerated up to 3 hours ahead of serving time.

fish pot pies

1 cup (250ml) fish stock

²/₃ cup (160ml) water

300g salmon fillets, cut into 2cm pieces

300g firm white fish fillets, cut into 2cm pieces

2 large potatoes (600g), chopped coarsely

1 small kumara (250g), chopped coarsely

2 tablespoons milk

40g butter

2 tablespoons plain flour

1 tablespoon finely chopped fresh flat-leaf parsley

½ cup (60g) coarsely grated cheddar cheese

1 Place stock and the water in medium saucepan; bring to the boil. Add fish; simmer until cooked. Place a few pieces of fish in 1 cup (250ml) shallow ovenproof dish for toddler, divide remaining fish into four shallow 1½-cup (375ml) ovenproof dishes. Strain stock into medium jug.

2 Boil, steam or microwave vegetables until tender; drain. Push vegetables through sieve into large bowl; stir in milk and half the butter until smooth. Preheat grill.

3 Melt remaining butter in small saucepan; add flour, cook, stirring, about 2 minutes or until mixture bubbles and thickens. Gradually stir in reserved stock mixture; cook, stirring, until sauce boils and thickens. Stir in parsley.

4 Pour a little sauce over toddler's fish; top with some vegetable mixture. Pour remaining sauce over fish in large dishes, top with remaining vegetable mixture; season.

5 Sprinkle dishes with cheese; grill until browned lightly.

prep + cook time 50 minutes **serves** 4

nutritional count per adult serving 21g total fat (10.7g saturated fat); 1969kJ (471 cal); 29.2g carbohydrate; 39.5g protein; 3.3g fibre

parmesan schnitzels
with kumara and broccoli mash

1 cup (100g) packaged breadcrumbs

½ cup (40g) finely grated parmesan cheese

¼ cup finely chopped fresh flat-leaf parsley

2 eggs

8 x 100g uncrumbed veal schnitzels

¼ cup (60ml) olive oil

2 medium kumara (800g), chopped coarsely

300g broccoli, chopped coarsely

20g butter

1 Combine breadcrumbs, cheese and parsley in medium shallow bowl. Whisk eggs in another medium shallow bowl. Coat schnitzels, one at a time, in egg then in breadcrumb mixture.

2 Heat half the oil in large frying pan; cook half the schnitzels until golden brown. Repeat with remaining oil and schnitzels.

3 Meanwhile, boil, steam or microwave vegetables, separately, until tender; drain. Mash vegetables with butter in medium bowl until almost smooth.

4 Cut part of a schnitzel into fingers for toddler; serve with some of the mash.

5 Divide remaining schnitzels onto serving plates, season to taste; serve with remaining mash.

prep + cook time 40 minutes **serves** 4

nutritional count per adult serving 27.8g total fat (8.5g saturated fat); 2805kJ (671 cal); 40.5g carbohydrate; 60.8g protein; 6.3g fibre

fish pot pies

tips The pies can be prepared several hours ahead, and instead of browning them under the grill, heat and brown them in the oven at 180°C/160°C fan-forced for about 30 minutes. The pies are not suitable to freeze.

tips Serve the schnitzels with a green salad and lemon wedges. The schnitzels can be crumbed then refrigerated several hours ahead of cooking. The mash is best made just before serving. Make sure you don't overcook the schnitzels.

parmesan schnitzels with kumara and broccoli mash

mixed berry yogurt

Crush ¼ cup thawed frozen mixed berries in small bowl with a fork; stir in ⅓ cup yogurt.

prep time 2 minutes **serves** 1

nutritional count per serving 3g total fat (1.9g saturated fat); 284kJ (68 cal); 5.2g carbohydrate; 4.7g protein; 0.9g fibre

muesli and honey yogurt

Combine ⅓ cup yogurt and 1 teaspoon honey in small bowl. Layer yogurt and 1 tablespoon toasted muesli in small serving dish.

note Honey may contain harmful bacteria and is not recommended for children under one year old.

prep time 5 minutes **serves** 1

nutritional count per serving 4.4g total fat (2.5g saturated fat); 501kJ (120 cal); 14.7g carbohydrate; 4.9g protein; 0.8g fibre

mango and passionfruit yogurt

Blend or process ½ cup yogurt and ¼ small coarsely chopped ripe mango until smooth. Serve yogurt drizzled with 2 teaspoons passionfruit pulp.

prep time 5 minutes **serves** 1

nutritional count per serving 4.6g total fat (2.8g saturated fat); 531kJ (127 cal); 13.9g carbohydrate; 6.9g protein; 2.2g fibre

banana and maple yogurt

Combine ½ cup yogurt and ½ teaspoon maple syrup in small bowl. Serve yogurt topped with ½ small thinly sliced ripe banana and another ½ teaspoon maple syrup.

prep time 5 minutes **serves** 1

nutritional count per serving 4.5g total fat (2.9g saturated fat); 619kJ (148 cal); 19.3g carbohydrate; 6.9g protein; 1g fibre

apple yogurt with cinnamon

Peel and coarsely grate ½ small fresh apple, then chop coarsely. Combine apple with ⅓ cup yogurt, 1 tablespoon sultanas and tiny pinch ground cinnamon in small bowl. Sprinkle with a little ground cinnamon, if you like.

prep time 5 minutes **serves** 1

nutritional count per serving 3g total fat (1.9g saturated fat); 552kJ (132 cal); 20.5g carbohydrate; 4.6g protein; 1.6g fibre

yogurt with dried fruit and coconut

Combine 1 tablespoon finely chopped dried apricots, 1 tablespoon finely chopped raisins and 1 teaspoon desiccated coconut in small bowl. Place ⅓ cup yogurt in serving bowl; sprinkle with apricot mixture.

prep time 5 minutes **serves** 1

nutritional count per serving 4g total fat (2.8g saturated fat); 552kJ (132 cal); 17.8g carbohydrate; 4.9g protein; 1.8g fibre

mixed berry yogurt

mango and passionfruit yogurt

yogurt snacks

Most kids like the texture of yogurt; it's perfect for introducing a variety of fruits and flavours to them.

muesli and honey yogurt

banana and maple yogurt

yogurt with dried fruit and coconut

apple yogurt with cinnamon

beef stir-fry with hokkien noodles

450g thin hokkien noodles

2 tablespoons peanut oil

700g beef rump steak, sliced thinly

1 medium red capsicum (200g), sliced thinly

100g button mushrooms, sliced thinly

3cm piece fresh ginger (15g), grated

2 cloves garlic, crushed

2 tablespoons hoisin sauce

2 tablespoons light soy sauce

4 green onions, sliced thickly

1 Place noodles in medium heatproof bowl, cover with boiling water; separate with fork, drain.

2 Heat half the oil in wok; stir-fry beef, in batches, until browned.

3 Heat remaining oil in wok; stir-fry capsicum, mushrooms, ginger and garlic until capsicum is tender.

4 Return beef to wok with noodles, sauces and onion; stir-fry until hot.

5 Coarsely chop some of the stir-fry for toddler. Divide remaining stir-fry onto serving plates.

prep + cook time 25 minutes **serves** 4

nutritional count per adult serving 22.9g total fat (7.2g saturated fat); 2880kJ (689 cal); 65g carbohydrate; 52.4g protein; 4.9g fibre

tip This is a last minute meal, although all the chopping can be done several hours ahead of stir-frying.

tips The pork can be prepared several hours ahead, ready for roasting; keep, covered, in the fridge. The potato mash is best made just before serving.

prosciutto and sage pork fillet

500g pork fillet

12 fresh sage leaves

8 slices prosciutto (90g)

1 tablespoon olive oil

800g potatoes, chopped coarsely

150g baby green beans, trimmed

¼ cup (60ml) hot milk

20g butter

1 Preheat oven to 220°C/200°C fan-forced.

2 Cut a small piece of pork from the fillet for the toddler; cut remaining pork into four equal-sized pieces. Place three sage leaves over each large piece of pork; then wrap each in two slices of prosciutto.

3 Heat oil in medium frying pan; cook pork, until browned all over. Place pork on baking-paper-lined oven tray. Roast, in oven, about 10 minutes or until cooked as desired. Remove from oven; stand 5 minutes. Slice prosciutto-wrapped pork thickly; cut toddler's pork into bite-sized pieces.

4 Meanwhile, boil, steam or microwave potato and beans, separately, until tender; drain. Push potato through sieve into large bowl; stir in milk and butter until smooth.

5 Serve toddler's pork with a little of the potato mash and some of the beans.

6 Divide remaining mash, beans and pork onto serving plates; season to taste.

prep + cook time 40 minutes (+ standing) **serves** 4

nutritional count per adult serving 13.7g total fat (5.2g saturated fat); 1568kJ (375 cal); 24g carbohydrate; 36.9g protein; 3.7g fibre

spaghetti with prawns and tomato

375g spaghetti

1 tablespoon olive oil

1 medium red onion (170g), chopped finely

2 cloves garlic, crushed

2 tablespoons tomato paste

700g bottled tomato pasta sauce

600g uncooked medium king prawns,
    shelled, deveined

½ cup (60g) seeded black olives

½ teaspoon dried chilli flakes

30g baby rocket leaves

1 Cook pasta in large saucepan of boiling water until tender; drain. Coarsely chop some of the pasta for toddler.

2 Meanwhile, heat oil in large saucepan; cook onion and garlic, stirring, until onion softens. Add paste; cook, stirring, 1 minute. Add sauce and prawns; bring to the boil. Reduce heat; simmer, uncovered, about 5 minutes or until prawns are cooked through.

3 Coarsely chop one prawn for toddler. Combine toddler's pasta, some of the sauce and chopped prawn in small bowl.

4 Add olives and chilli to remaining sauce, season to taste; cook, stirring, until heated through. Add remaining pasta; stir to coat in sauce. Divide into serving bowls; top with rocket.

prep + cook time 30 minutes **serves** 4

nutritional count per adult serving 7.6g total fat (1.1g saturated fat); 2332kJ (558 cal); 87.5g carbohydrate; 29.6g protein; 7.8g fibre

tip This recipe is best made as close to serving time as possible as prawns toughen on reheating.

food to cope with allergies

The sweet and savoury recipes (the pastry is a real winner) in this chapter are suitable for a variety of food intolerances. Read the recipes carefully to make sure the ingredients meet your child's needs.

savoury buckwheat pancakes
(wheat-free, gluten-free & nut-free)

1 cup (150g) buckwheat flour
½ cup (60g) gluten-free plain flour
3 teaspoons gluten-free baking powder
2 eggs
2 cups (500ml) buttermilk
50g butter, melted
1 medium zucchini (120g), grated coarsely
1 small carrot (70g), grated coarsely
½ cup (80g) fresh or frozen corn kernels

1 Sift flours and baking powder into large bowl; gradually whisk in combined eggs and buttermilk until smooth. Stir in butter and vegetables.
2 Heat lightly oiled small frying pan; pour ⅓ cup of the batter into pan. Cook pancake until bubbles appear on surface. Turn pancake; cook until browned lightly. Repeat with remaining batter.
prep + cook time 30 minutes **makes** 10
nutritional count per pancake 8.1g total fat (2g saturated fat); 1388kJ (332 cal); 38.2g carbohydrate; 23.5g protein; 5.4g fibre

tip You will need about half a corn cob (200g) for this recipe. Pancakes are delicious plain, but could also be served with shredded chicken and a mild mango chutney (be sure to check the label, or use home-made chutney). Pancakes are not suitable to freeze, but can be made a day ahead.

macaroni cheese with peas
(dairy-free, gluten-free, nut-free
& wheat-free)

250g packet gluten-free spiral pasta
2 tablespoons dairy-free spread
2 tablespoons cornflour (100% corn)
1½ cups (375ml) water
1 cup (250ml) soy milk
½ cup (60g) coarsely grated soya cheese
1 cup (120g) frozen baby peas
½ cup (35g) stale gluten-free breadcrumbs

1 Preheat oven to 200°C/180°C fan-forced.

2 Cook pasta in large saucepan of boiling water until tender; drain.

3 Meanwhile, melt spread in large saucepan, stir in cornflour; cook, stirring, 1 minute. Gradually add the combined water and milk, stirring constantly, until mixture boils and thickens slightly. Remove from heat; stir in cheese, peas and pasta.

4 Pour mixture into oiled shallow 1.5-litre (6-cup) ovenproof dish; sprinkle with breadcrumbs. Bake about 25 minutes. Cool before serving.

prep + cook time 50 minutes serves 6
nutritional count per serving 10.4g total fat
(1.4g saturated fat); 1200kJ (287 cal); 35.1g carbohydrate;
10.1g protein; 5.5g fibre

tip This recipe is best made and eaten as soon as it's cool enough; it's not suitable to freeze.

tip Quesadillas are best made and eaten as soon as they're cool enough to handle. They are not suitable to freeze.

quesadillas

(dairy-free, egg-free & nut-free)

2 medium tomatoes (300g), seeded, chopped finely
1 medium avocado (250g), chopped finely
1 medium zucchini (120g), grated coarsely
½ small red onion (50g), chopped finely
125g can corn kernels, rinsed, drained
425g can mexe-style beans, rinsed, drained
1 cup (130g) coarsely grated soya cheese
8 small corn tortillas (280g)

1 Preheat sandwich press.
2 Combine vegetables and beans in medium bowl.
3 Divide bean mixture and the cheese over four tortillas, leaving 2cm border around edge; top each with the remaining tortillas.
4 Cook quesadillas, one at a time, in sandwich press until browned lightly. Cut into quarters.

prep + cook time 30 minutes **makes** 4
nutritional count per quesadilla 19.8g total fat
(2.9g saturated fat); 1413kJ (338 cal); 22.6g carbohydrate;
13.8g protein; 7.8g fibre

semi-dried tomato and spinach tart
(wheat-free, gluten-free & nut-free)

300ml light thickened cream

2 tablespoons milk

4 eggs

½ cup (80g) coarsely shredded cooked chicken

¼ cup (35g) drained semi-dried tomatoes,
   chopped finely

25g baby spinach leaves, torn coarsely

gluten-free pastry

1 cup (180g) rice flour

¼ cup (35g) cornflour (100% corn)

¼ cup (30g) soya flour

170g cold butter, chopped coarsely

2 tablespoons cold water, approximately

1 Make gluten-free pastry.

2 Preheat oven to 220°C/200°C fan-forced. Grease
11cm x 34cm loose-based fluted flan tin with melted butter.

3 Roll pastry between sheets of baking paper until 5mm
thick. Ease pastry into tin, press into base and sides; trim
edge, prick base with fork.

4 Bake pastry case about 15 minutes or until browned
lightly. Cool pastry case. Reduce oven temperature to
200°C/180°C fan-forced.

5 Meanwhile, whisk cream, milk and eggs in medium jug.
Fill pastry case with chicken, tomato and spinach; pour in
the egg mixture. Bake tart about 25 minutes.

gluten-free pastry Process flours and butter until mixture
is crumbly. Add enough of the water to make ingredients
come together. Knead dough gently and lightly on floured
surface until smooth.

prep + cook time 1 hour 10 minutes **serves** 10

nutritional count per serving 31.3g total fat
(19.3g saturated fat); 1693kJ (405 cal); 22.2g carbohydrate;
8.5g protein; 1.4g fibre

tips We found it necessary to grease the tin well with butter. The tart is best made and eaten warm or cold on the same day; it is not suitable to freeze. The pastry can be made 2 days ahead, and refrigerated, or frozen for up to a month.

cheesy corn and chicken loaves

tips You will need about 1 corn cob (400g) for this recipe. Serve loaves with steamed mixed vegetables. Loaves can be served warm or cold. They can be made a day ahead, but are not suitable to freeze.

tip Accompany with lemon wedges. This recipe is best made, cooked and eaten as soon as it's cool enough.

rice-crumbed fish and chips

cheesy corn and chicken loaves
(wheat-free, gluten-free & nut-free)

$^1/_3$ cup (6g) puffed millet
900g chicken mince
1 clove garlic, crushed
1 egg
¾ cup (120g) fresh or frozen corn kernels
½ cup (60g) coarsely grated cheddar cheese
¼ cup coarsely chopped fresh chives

1 Preheat oven to 220°C/200°C fan-forced. Grease 8-hole ½ cup (125ml) petite loaf pan.
2 Blend or process millet until fine.
3 Combine mince, garlic, egg, corn, cheese, millet and 2 tablespoons of the chives in large bowl. Divide mixture into pan holes.
4 Bake loaves 10 minutes; remove from oven. Sprinkle with remaining chives. Bake a further 10 minutes or until cooked through.

prep + cook time 35 minutes **makes** 8
nutritional count per loaf 12.5g total fat (4.5g saturated fat); 949kJ (227 cal); 3.1g carbohydrate; 25.1g protein; 0.8g fibre
note If you have one, the millet is best processed in a small processor bowl.

rice-crumbed fish and chips
(wheat-free, gluten-free, egg-free & dairy-free)

1 medium potato (200g)
$^1/_3$ cup (20g) rice flakes
2 teaspoons finely chopped fresh flat-leaf parsley
1 teaspoon finely grated lemon rind
180g firm white fish fillet, halved lengthways
cooking-oil spray

1 Preheat oven to 220°C/200°C fan-forced.
2 Cut potato into 1cm slices; cut slices into 1cm chips. Place chips on baking-paper-lined oven tray; bake about 35 minutes or until browned lightly.
3 Meanwhile, coarsely crush rice flakes in small bowl; mix in parsley and rind. Press crumb mixture onto both sides of fish; spray fish with cooking-oil spray for about 2 seconds each side.
4 Place fish on tray; cook fish in oven for final 10 minutes of chip-cooking time.
5 Divide fish and chips between two serving plates.

prep + cook time 1 hour **serves** 2
nutritional count per serving 6g total fat (0.9g saturated fat); 919kJ (220 cal); 19g carbohydrate; 21.3g protein; 1.9g fibre
note Rice flakes are available from health-food stores and most supermarkets.

apple turnovers

(wheat-free, gluten-free & egg-free)

2 medium apples (300g), peeled, chopped finely

1 teaspoon caster sugar

2 tablespoons water

1 teaspoon pure icing sugar

gluten-free pastry

1¼ cups (225g) rice flour

¼ cup (35g) cornflour (100% corn)

¼ cup (30g) soya flour

⅓ cup (75g) caster sugar

150g cold butter, chopped coarsely

2 tablespoons cold water, approximately

1 Preheat oven to 200°C/180°C fan-forced. Grease and line oven tray with baking paper.

2 Make gluten-free pastry.

3 Combine apple, sugar and the water in small saucepan; bring to the boil. Reduce heat; simmer, covered, about 5 minutes or until apple is tender. Cool.

4 Roll pastry lightly between sheets of baking paper until 5mm thick; cut 18 x 8cm rounds from pastry. Drop heaped teaspoons of apple mixture into centre of each round; fold to enclose filling, pinching edges to seal. Place turnovers on tray.

5 Bake turnovers, in oven, about 15 minutes; cool on trays. Serve dusted with sifted icing sugar.

gluten-free pastry Process flours, sugar and butter until crumbly. Add enough of the water to make ingredients come together. Knead dough gently and lightly on floured surface until smooth.

prep + cook time 40 minutes **makes** 18

nutritional count per turnover 7.2g total fat (4.6g saturated fat); 631kJ (151 cal); 19.6g carbohydrate; 1.7g protein; 0.7g fibre

tips Stewed apple and pastry can be prepared 2 days ahead; keep covered in the fridge. Turnovers can be made two days ahead, keep in an airtight container at room temperature. Turnovers are not suitable to freeze.

berry crumbles with frozen yogurt
(gluten-free, yeast-free, wheat-free & egg-free)

1 cup (150g) fresh or frozen mixed berries
2 tablespoons strawberry-flavoured frozen yogurt
crumble topping
2 tablespoons puffed rice
1 tablespoon gluten-free plain flour
1 tablespoon brown rice flour
1 tablespoon brown sugar
15g butter

1 Preheat oven to 200°C/180°C fan-forced. Grease two ¾ cup (180ml) ovenproof dishes.
2 Make crumble topping.
3 Divide berries into dishes; sprinkle with crumble topping. Bake about 30 minutes or until browned lightly.
4 Serve crumbles warm with frozen yogurt.
crumble topping Blend or process puffed rice until fine. Add flours, sugar and butter; process until crumbly.
prep + cook time 50 minutes makes 2
nutritional count per crumble 8.2g total fat (5.2g saturated fat); 911kJ (218 cal); 31.2g carbohydrate; 3.5g protein; 2.2g fibre

saucy caramel pudding
(wheat-free, gluten-free & egg-free)

1 cup (135g) gluten-free self-raising flour
$^1/_3$ cup (75g) firmly packed brown sugar
20g butter, melted
½ cup (125ml) milk
caramel sauce
1$^1/_3$ cups (330ml) water
$^1/_3$ cup (75g) firmly packed brown sugar
30g butter

1 Preheat oven to 180°C/160°C fan-forced. Grease deep 1-litre (4-cup) ovenproof dish.
2 Combine sifted flour, sugar, butter and milk in medium bowl. Pour mixture into dish.
3 Make caramel sauce.
4 Pour sauce slowly over back of spoon evenly into mixture in dish. Bake pudding about 50 minutes. Stand 10 minutes before serving.
caramel sauce Combine ingredients in small saucepan; stir over medium heat, without boiling, until smooth.
prep + cook time 1 hour 10 minutes **serves** 4
nutritional count per serving 11.7g total fat (7.6g saturated fat); 1208kJ (289 cal); 67.1g carbohydrate; 1.7g protein; 0.5g fibre

chocolate-on-chocolate cakes
(gluten-free, yeast-free & wheat-free)

200g butter, softened
2¼ cups (300g) gluten-free self-raising flour
¼ cup (25g) cocoa powder
1 cup (220g) caster sugar
¾ cup (180ml) milk
2 eggs
2 egg whites
chocolate icing
1 cup (160g) pure icing sugar
1 tablespoon cocoa powder
2 tablespoons water

1 Preheat oven to 180°C/160°C fan-forced. Line two 12-hole ($^1/_3$-cup/80ml) muffin pans with paper cases.
2 Beat butter in large bowl with electric mixer until pale. Beat sifted flour, cocoa and ¼ cup of the caster sugar alternately with milk into butter, in two batches, until combined.
3 Beat eggs and egg whites in small bowl with electric mixer until thick and creamy. Gradually add remaining caster sugar, one tablespoon at a time, beating until sugar dissolves between additions. Gradually beat egg mixture into flour mixture until combined.
4 Drop 2½ tablespoons mixture into each paper case; bake cakes about 20 minutes. Turn, top-side-up, onto wire rack to cool.
5 Meanwhile, make chocolate icing. Spread cold cakes with chocolate icing.
chocolate icing Sift sugar and cocoa into small bowl; stir in water.
prep + cook time 40 minutes (+ cooling) **makes** 24
nutritional count per cake 7.8g total fat (4.9g saturated fat); 635kJ (152 cal); 27.4g carbohydrate; 1.6g protein; 0.2g fibre
storage Store cakes in an airtight container for up to two days. Uniced cakes can be frozen for up to two months.

saucy caramel pudding

tips Serve pudding with cream or ice-cream. Puddings can be made in either texas muffin pans or individual ovenproof dishes – they will take about 20 minutes to cook. This recipe can be made up to 4 hours ahead of serving and is best served warm; pudding is not suitable to freeze.

chocolate-on-chocolate cakes

tip For a dairy-free version of this cake, substitute dairy-free spread for the butter, and soy milk for the milk; the rest of the recipe stays the same.

healthy parties

It's a challenge to convince kids to eat healthy food at a party – but not with these recipes. The food looks good and tastes wonderful and, what's more, most of the food in this chapter is portable.

berry punch

250g strawberries
1 litre (4 cups) tropical fruit punch juice
1 litre (4 cups) chilled dry ginger ale
125g blueberries
125g raspberries
2 teaspoons grenadine-flavoured syrup

1 Finely chop half the strawberries. Divide into holes of 12-hole (1-tablespoon/20ml) ice-cube tray. Pour 1 cup of the juice into the holes; freeze 3 hours or overnight.
2 Coarsely chop remaining strawberries; combine in large punch bowl or jug with remaining juice, ginger ale, strawberry ice-cubes, blueberries, raspberries and grenadine.
prep time 15 minutes (+ freezing) **makes** 2 litres
nutritional count per ½ cup (125ml) 0.2g total fat (0g saturated fat); 236kJ (56 cal); 19g carbohydrate; 0.5g protein; 0.9g fibre
tip We used the grenadine cordial to add some colour to the punch; you can use any cordial you like, however, the colour may not be as intense as that of the grenadine.

tips The strawberry ice-blocks can be made at least a week before the party. Finish the punch as close to serving as possible.

lamb kofta sticks

500g lamb mince
1 egg
1 small brown onion (80g), chopped finely
½ teaspoon ground cinnamon
1 tablespoon finely chopped fresh flat-leaf parsley
½ cup (140g) yogurt

1 Combine lamb, egg, onion, cinnamon and parsley in medium bowl.
2 Shape level tablespoons of lamb mixture into sausage shapes on 24 ice-block sticks; flatten slightly.
3 Cook kofta sticks, in batches, in heated oiled large frying pan until cooked through. Serve with yogurt.

prep + cook time 35 minutes **makes** 24
nutritional count per kofta stich 7.7g total fat (3.6g saturated fat); 568kJ (136 cal); 1.4g carbohydrate; 15.2g protein; 0.2g fibre

tips You need to soak 24 ice-block sticks in cold water for 1 hour to prevent scorching during cooking.
Kofta can be made and shaped onto the sticks a day ahead of the party; keep covered in the fridge. Uncooked kofta can be frozen for up to two months; thaw them in the fridge the night before the party.

toastie men

14 slices white bread (630g)
14 slices wholemeal bread (630g)
250g spreadable cream cheese
70g shaved ham, chopped finely
1 tablespoon finely chopped fresh chives
95g can tuna in springwater, drained
1 tablespoon finely chopped cornichons
1 tablespoon finely chopped fresh flat-leaf parsley

1 Preheat grill.
2 Using gingerbread man cutter, cut three 5cm men from each slice of bread; place on oven trays. Toast bread, in batches, under grill until browned both sides.
3 Divide cream cheese into two small bowls; stir ham and chives into one bowl, and stir tuna, cornichons and parsley into remaining bowl.
4 Spread level teaspoons of ham mixture onto each white toast; spread level teaspoons of tuna mixture onto each wholemeal toast.

prep + cook time 45 minutes makes 42 of each
nutritional count per toastie man 1.5g total fat
(0.7g saturated fat); 201kJ (48 cal); 6.3g carbohydrate;
2.1g protein; 0.7g fibre

tips You can make toasts one day ahead and store in an airtight container. Make fillings one day ahead and store, covered, in the refrigerator. Assemble the toastie men several hours before the party.

roasted vegie and ricotta bread

1 medium zucchini (120g), sliced thinly lengthways

1 small french bread stick (150g)

½ cup (120g) ricotta cheese

2 slices roasted eggplant (125g)

4 slices roasted red capsicum (170g)

½ cup (30g) finely shredded iceberg lettuce

1 Cook zucchini on heated oiled grill plate (or grill or barbecue) until tender. Cool.

2 Cut down centre of bread stick, without cutting all the way through. Open bread stick; remove soft bread inside, leaving 1cm-thick shell.

3 Spread cheese inside bread stick. Layer eggplant, capsicum, zucchini and lettuce inside bread case. Wrap bread stick tightly in plastic wrap.

4 Place bread stick on tray; top with another tray, weight with a small can. Refrigerate 3 hours before cutting.

prep + cook time 30 minutes (+ refrigeration) makes 16

nutritional count per slice 3.8g total fat (0.9g saturated fat); 270kJ (65 cal); 5.5g carbohydrate; 2g protein; 0.5g fibre

spaghetti bolognese baskets

150g angel hair spaghetti

1 egg

¼ cup (20g) finely grated parmesan cheese

2 teaspoons olive oil

1 stalk celery (150g), trimmed, chopped finely

1 small carrot (70g), chopped finely

1 small brown onion (80g), chopped finely

200g beef mince

1 tablespoon tomato paste

1 cup (260g) bottled tomato pasta sauce

36 small basil leaves

1 Preheat oven to 180°C/160°C fan-forced. Grease three 12-hole (1-tablespoon/20ml) round-based patty pans.

2 Cook pasta in large saucepan of boiling water until tender; drain. Cool.

3 Combine pasta, egg and cheese in medium bowl; divide pasta mixture into pan holes, press the mixture firmly to cover pan holes evenly.

4 Bake pasta baskets about 20 minutes or until set. Cool in pans.

5 Meanwhile, heat oil in medium frying pan. Cook vegetables, stirring, until soft. Add beef, cook, stirring, until browned. Add paste and sauce; bring to the boil. Reduce heat; simmer, uncovered, about 10 minutes or until bolognese thickens.

6 Remove pasta baskets from pan using metal spatula; transfer to serving plate. Divide bolognese into baskets; top each with a basil leaf.

prep + cook time 45 minutes makes 36

nutritional count per basket 1.2g total fat (0.4g saturated fat); 148kJ (35 cal); 3.8g carbohydrate; 2.1g protein; 0.4g fibre

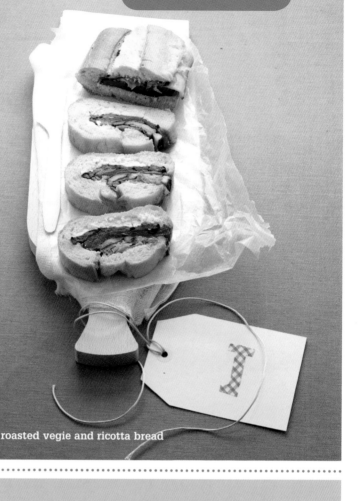

roasted vegie and ricotta bread

tips The bread stick can be prepared up to 12 hours before the party. Keep it wrapped and weighted in the fridge. Slice the stick as close to serving time as possible. Roasted zucchini, eggplant and capsicum can be bought loose from delis, making the job even easier.

spaghetti bolognese baskets

tips The pasta cases can be made, cooled, and removed from the pans one day before the party. Store in an airtight container at room temperature. The bolognese sauce can be made 2 days ahead; keep, covered, in the fridge, or freeze for several months. Assemble the baskets up to 3 hours before the party.

tips Serve with child-friendly sweet chilli or soy sauce for dipping. The rolls can be made a day before the party; keep covered with damp absorbent paper, then plastic wrap, in the fridge. Bake the rolls up to an hour before serving.

chicken spring rolls

mini vegie burgers

tips Patties can be made a day before the party; keep them covered in the fridge. The sauce can be made a week before the party; keep covered in the fridge. Assemble the burgers up to 3 hours before the party.

chicken spring rolls

2 cups (500ml) water
200g chicken breast fillet
1 medium carrot (120g), grated coarsely
½ cup (40g) bean sprouts, chopped finely
1 tablespoon finely chopped fresh coriander
1 tablespoon light soy sauce
50 wonton wrappers

1 Bring the water to the boil in small saucepan; add chicken. Reduce heat; simmer, covered, about 10 minutes or until chicken is cooked through. Cool chicken in poaching liquid 10 minutes; drain, shred chicken finely using two forks.
2 Preheat oven to 220°C/200°C fan-forced. Grease and line oven tray with baking paper.
3 Combine chicken, carrot, sprouts, coriander and sauce in medium bowl.
4 Place rounded teaspoons of chicken mixture along bottom edge of each wrapper. Fold in sides then moisten top edge with water; roll to enclose filling, place on tray.
5 Bake about 15 minutes or until rolls are browned lightly and crisp.
prep + cook time 45 minutes **makes** 50
nutritional count per roll 0.3g total fat
(0g saturated fat); 48kJ (12 cal); 0.3g carbohydrate;
1.8g protein; 0g fibre
note You'll need to buy 2 x 270g packets of wonton wrappers. They are available from the refrigerated section of Asian grocery stores and most supermarkets.

mini vegie burgers

12 small par-baked white dinner rolls (300g)
2 medium potatoes (400g), chopped coarsely
1 small carrot (70g), grated coarsely
1 medium tomato (150g), seeded, chopped finely
2 green onions, chopped finely
1 egg white
½ cup (50g) packaged breadcrumbs
⅓ cup (40g) coarsely grated cheddar cheese
1 cup (60g) finely shredded iceberg lettuce
barbecue sauce
¼ cup (60ml) tomato sauce
1 tablespoon cider vinegar
2 teaspoons worcestershire sauce
1 tablespoon brown sugar
2 teaspoons american-style mustard

1 Bake bread rolls following packet instructions.
2 Meanwhile, boil, steam or microwave potato until tender; drain. Push potato through sieve into medium bowl; stir in carrot, tomato, onion, egg white, breadcrumbs and cheese. Shape level tablespoons of mixture into 24 patties; place on baking-paper-lined tray. Cover, refrigerate 1 hour.
3 Meanwhile, make barbecue sauce.
4 Cook patties in heated oiled large frying pan until browned both sides.
5 Split rolls in half horizontally; cut each roll in half crossways. You will have 24 mini burger buns. Divide patties, lettuce and barbecue sauce between buns.
barbecue sauce Combine ingredients in small saucepan; bring to the boil. Reduce heat; simmer, uncovered, stirring occasionally, about 10 minutes or until thickened.
prep + cook time 50 minutes (+ refrigeration) **makes** 24
nutritional count per burger 1.2g total fat
(0.4g saturated fat); 287kJ (69 cal); 11.4g carbohydrate;
2.5g protein; 1g fibre

pesto mushroom cups

24 button mushrooms (300g)
½ cup (130g) bottled basil pesto
12 cherry tomatoes (100g), halved
½ cup (60g) coarsely grated cheddar cheese
24 small basil leaves

1 Remove stalks from mushrooms; place top-side down on foiled-lined tray. Divide pesto into mushroom cups; top each with a tomato half, cut-side up, sprinkle with cheese.
2 Preheat grill.
3 Grill mushrooms about 5 minutes or until cheese melts. Serve each topped with a basil leaf.

prep + cook time 25 minutes **makes** 24

nutritional count per mushroom cup 3g total fat (1g saturated fat); 146kJ (35 cal); 0.2g carbohydrate; 1.6g protein; 0.5g fibre

tips Prepare the mushrooms, ready for grilling the day before the party; keep covered in the fridge. Mushrooms can be grilled up to 30 minutes before serving.

polenta and avocado bites

3 cups (750ml) water

¾ cup (120g) polenta

½ cup (60g) coarsely grated cheddar cheese

1 medium avocado (250g)

2 teaspoons lemon juice

1 tablespoon olive oil

18 grape tomatoes (145g), halved

1 Oil deep 20cm-square cake pan.

2 Place the water in medium saucepan; bring to the boil. Gradually stir polenta into the water. Reduce heat; simmer, stirring, about 10 minutes or until polenta thickens. Stir in cheese; spread polenta into pan, cool 10 minutes. Cover; refrigerate 1 hour or until polenta is firm.

3 Mash avocado and juice in small bowl until mixture is almost smooth.

4 Turn polenta onto board; cut polenta into 36 squares. Heat oil in large frying pan; cook polenta, turning, until browned all over.

5 Top polenta squares with avocado mixture, then tomatoes.

prep + cook time 35 minutes (+ refrigeration) **makes** 36 **nutritional count per bite** 2.2g total fat (0.7g saturated fat); 138kJ (33 cal); 2.4g carbohydrate; 0.8g protein; 0.2g fibre

tips The polenta can be made and kept, in the pan, in the fridge for up to 2 days before the party. The squares can be completed up to 2 hours before the party.

sticky chicken drumettes

¾ cup (180ml) tomato sauce

⅓ cup (80ml) plum sauce

2 tablespoons worcestershire sauce

1 tablespoon brown sugar

16 chicken drumettes (1kg)

1 Combine sauces and sugar in large bowl; add chicken. Cover; refrigerate 3 hours or overnight.

2 Preheat oven to 200°C/180°C fan-forced.

3 Drain chicken; discard marinade. Place chicken on oiled wire rack over large baking dish. Roast chicken about 30 minutes or until cooked through.

prep + cook time 40 minutes (+ refrigeration) **makes** 16

nutritional count per drumette 3.8g total fat (1.1g saturated fat); 380kJ (91 cal); 7.8g carbohydrate; 6.2g protein; 0.3g fibre

chicken and vegie rice paper rolls

1 large carrot (180g), grated coarsely

2 stalks celery (300g), trimmed, chopped finely

150g wombok, shredded finely

1½ cups (240g) finely shredded cooked chicken

½ cup (40g) bean sprouts, chopped coarsely

2 tablespoons lemon juice

1 tablespoon fish sauce

2 teaspoons brown sugar

24 x 17cm-square rice paper sheets

24 fresh mint leaves

1 Combine carrot, celery, wombok, chicken, sprouts, juice, sauce and sugar in medium bowl.

2 Place one sheet of rice paper in medium bowl of warm water until just softened. Lift sheet from water carefully; place on a tea-towel-covered board with a corner pointing towards you.

3 Place 1 rounded tablespoon of vegetable mixture horizontally in centre of sheet; top with one mint leaf. Fold corner facing you over filling; roll to cover filling, then fold in sides. Continue rolling to enclose filling. Repeat with remaining rice paper sheets, vegetable mixture and mint leaves.

prep time 35 minutes **makes** 24

nutritional count per roll 0.9g total fat (0.2g saturated fat); 196kJ (47 cal); 6g carbohydrate; 3.3g protein; 0.7g fibre

sticky chicken drumettes

tips Marinate the chicken up to a day before the party. Roast the chicken up to an hour before serving – don't forget to deal with the guest's small sticky fingers.

tips Serve the rice paper rolls with a mild sweet chilli sauce or soy sauce. Prepare the rolls up to 3 hours before the party; keep them on a tray, in a single layer, in the fridge, covered with a damp tea towel.

chicken and vegie rice paper rolls

tips Once you have dipped the calamari rings in egg white, thread the rings onto a wooden spoon handle and roll the outside surface only in breadcrumbs. Completely coating the rings will make them soggy in the centre after baking. It's important to cook the squid at a high temperature, but it can easily overcook and toughen. It might be necessary to remove smaller pieces of squid from the trays as they cook. Cook the squid as close to serving time as possible as it's best served warm. Make the sauce the day before the party; keep it covered in the fridge.

oven-baked calamari

500g cleaned squid hoods

2 egg whites

¾ cup (75g) packaged wholemeal breadcrumbs

buttermilk dipping sauce

2 tablespoons buttermilk

2 tablespoons mayonnaise

1 tablespoon finely chopped cornichons

2 teaspoons lemon juice

1 teaspoon finely chopped fresh flat-leaf parsley

1 Preheat oven to 250°C/230°C fan-forced. Grease and line two oven trays with baking paper.

2 Cut squid into 2cm-thick rings. Dip rings in egg white, then roll outside surface of rings in breadcrumbs. Place rings, in single layer, on trays; bake about 5 minutes or until squid is tender.

3 Meanwhile, make buttermilk dipping sauce.

4 Serve calamari with buttermilk dipping sauce; accompany with lemon wedges.

buttermilk dipping sauce Combine ingredients in small bowl.

prep + cook time 20 minutes serves 8

nutritional count per serving 2.7g total fat (0.5g saturated fat); 410kJ (98 cal); 5.4g carbohydrate; 12.5g protein; 0.7g fibre

tropical jelly cups

1 tablespoon powdered gelatine
¼ cup (60ml) water
2¾ cups (680ml) tropical fruit juice
tropical salsa
1 medium banana (200g), chopped finely
½ medium mango (215g), chopped finely
¼ cup (60ml) passionfruit pulp

1 Sprinkle gelatine over the water in small heatproof jug;
stand in small saucepan of simmering water, stirring, until
gelatine dissolves.
2 Combine juice and gelatine mixture in large jug;
pour ¼ cup (60ml) mixture into 12 x ½-cup (125ml)
serving cups. Cover, refrigerate 3 hours or until set.
3 Make tropical salsa.
4 Just before serving, spoon level tablespoons of salsa
into each cup.
tropical salsa Combine ingredients in a small bowl.
prep + cook time 20 minutes (+ refrigeration) **makes** 12
nutritional count per jelly cup 0.2g total fat
(0g saturated fat); 201kJ (48 cal); 9.5g carbohydrate;
1.4g protein; 1.1g fibre

teddy bear biscuits

200g unsalted butter, softened
1 teaspoon vanilla extract
¾ cup (165g) caster sugar
1 egg
40g dark eating chocolate, grated finely
1¼ cups (175g) plain flour
2 tablespoons cocoa powder
24 mini M&M's
12 dark chocolate Melts

1 Preheat oven to 180°C/160°C fan-forced. Grease three
oven trays; line with baking paper.
2 Beat butter, extract, sugar and egg in small bowl with
electric mixer until just changed to a paler colour; do
not overbeat. Stir in chocolate, sifted flour and cocoa.
Refrigerate 15 minutes.
3 Roll 24 level teaspoons of the mixture into balls. Roll
remaining mixture into 12 large balls for teddy faces. On
each tray, flatten four large balls with palm of hand to
form an 8cm-diameter circle. Position two small balls on
top of each circle for ears. Flatten balls with palm of hand.
Slide one ice-block stick two-thirds of the way into dough
in each face.
4 Position M&M's into dough for eyes and Melts for nose.
5 Bake biscuits about 12 minutes or until browned lightly.
Cool on trays.
prep + cook time 50 minutes (+ refrigeration) **makes** 12
nutritional count per biscuit 16g total fat
(10.4g saturated fat); 1134kJ (272 cal); 29.4g carbohydrate;
2.3g protein; 0.7g fibre

tropical jelly cups

tips You need 3 passionfruit for this recipe. The jelly cups can be made a day before the party. The salsa is best made an hour before serving.

eddy bear biscuits

tips Every child deserves at least one treat at a party and, while we know these gorgeous Teddy Bear biscuits are not very healthy, we decided to include them as their special occasion treat. Just make sure each child only eats one. You need 12 wooden ice-block sticks for this recipe.

caramel banana tart

1 sheet puff pastry
20g butter
2 tablespoons brown sugar
pinch ground cinnamon
2 medium bananas (400g), sliced thinly

1 Preheat oven to 220°C/200°C fan-forced.

2 Place pastry on an oiled oven tray. Fold edges of pastry over to make a 1cm border all the way around pastry. Prick pastry base with fork. Place another oven tray on top of pastry (this stops the pastry from puffing up during baking); bake 10 minutes. Remove top tray from pastry.

3 Meanwhile, combine butter, sugar and cinnamon in small saucepan; stir over low heat until smooth. Combine butter mixture and banana in medium bowl.

4 Top tart with banana mixture. Bake about 10 minutes. Cool 20 minutes before cutting.

prep + cook time 30 minutes **serves** 16

nutritional count per serving 3.4g total fat (1.9g saturated fat); 296kJ (71 cal); 8.8g carbohydrate; 0.9g protein; 0.5g fibre

tips Serve with caramel sauce and whipped cream or ice-cream. The tart can be made up to 3 hours before the party, but it is good eaten warm. The pastry case can be baked 2 days before the party; keep it in an airtight container at room temperature, then fill it with the banana mixture just before the final baking.

apple and blackcurrant jellies

Combine 1½ cups apple and blackcurrant juice and 1 tablespoon caster sugar in small saucepan; stir over low heat until sugar dissolves. Place ¼ cup water in small heatproof jug; sprinkle over 3 teaspoons powdered gelatine. Stand jug in small saucepan of simmering water; stir until gelatine dissolves. Stir gelatine mixture into juice mixture. Rinse inside of four ½ cup (125ml) moulds with water; divide mixture into moulds. Divide 1 small peeled, finely chopped apple between moulds. Cover; refrigerate overnight. Wipe outside of moulds with hot cloth. Turn jellies onto plates.

prep + cook time 15 minutes (+ refrigeration) **makes** 4

nutritional count per jelly 0g total fat (0g saturated fat); 339kJ (81 cal); 17.5g carbohydrate; 22g protein; 0.5g fibre

tip Jellies are at their best made one day ahead; they are not suitable to freeze.

starry melon wands

Cut 1.5kg piece seedless watermelon and 800g piece honeydew melon into 1.5cm slices. Cut out 7.5cm stars from watermelon. Cut out 4cm stars from the centres of these stars. Cut out ten 4cm stars from honeydew melon slices. Place the honeydew stars in the centre of each watermelon star. Cut off the bendy end from 10 plastic straws, push a straw through the centre of one side of the joined stars to hold the small star in position. Repeat with remaining melons and straws. Combine 1 teaspoon honey and 1 cup yogurt in small bowl to use for dipping.

prep time 25 minutes **makes** 10

nutritional count per wand 1g total fat (0.3g saturated fat); 347kJ (83 cal); 15.3g carbohydrate; 2.3g protein; 1.7g fibre

tips Freeze the fruit wands to make healthy ice-blocks. You can also make wands out of the remaining small watermelon stars.
Honey may contain harmful bacteria and is not recommended for children under one year old.

starry melon wands

muesli lunchbox cookies

Preheat oven to 180°C/160°C fan-forced. Grease oven trays; line with baking paper. Beat 250g softened butter and 1¼ cups firmly packed brown sugar in small bowl with electric mixer until light and fluffy. Beat in 1 egg and ¼ cup milk until combined; transfer mixture to large bowl. Stir in sifted 1¼ cups plain flour and ½ teaspoon bicarbonate of soda, 3½ cups fruit and cereal snack mix (see page 48) and 2 cups rolled oats until combined. Drop rounded tablespoons of mixture onto trays about 4cm apart. Bake cookies about 15 minutes. Stand on trays 5 minutes before transferring to wire rack to cool.

prep + cook time 1 hour 10 minutes **makes** about 50

nutritional count per cookie 4.7g total fat (3.1g saturated fat); 359kJ (86 cal); 9.7g carbohydrate; 1g protein; 0.8g fibre

tip Cookies will keep in an airtight container for a week, or they can be frozen for up to 2 months.

treats + desserts

Kids and adults alike love to end a meal with a sweet treat, and these delicious recipes have an added bonus of a healthy twist.

apple and blackcurrant jellies

muesli lunchbox cookies

rhubarb, apple and pear crumble

Preheat oven to 200°C/180°C fan-forced. Coarsely chop 3 trimmed stalks rhubarb, 2 medium peeled apples and 1 small peeled pear and combine with ¼ cup water in medium saucepan; bring to the boil. Simmer, covered, stirring occasionally, about 10 minutes or until fruit is tender. Combine ¼ cup plain flour, ¼ cup rolled oats and 2 tablespoons brown sugar in small bowl; rub in 30g chopped butter. Spoon fruit mixture into greased deep 1-litre (4-cup) ovenproof dish; sprinkle with oat mixture. Bake about 30 minutes or until browned lightly.

prep + cook time 45 minutes **serves** 4

nutritional count per serving 6.9g total fat (4.2g saturated fat); 828kJ (198 cal); 29.2g carbohydrate; 2.6g protein; 4g fibre

tip Make crumbles in individual dishes; freeze for up to 2 months before baking.

ricotta and honey crêpes

Sift ½ cup plain flour into small bowl; whisk in combined 1 cup milk and 1 egg until smooth. Strain batter into medium jug; stand 30 minutes. Combine 250g ricotta cheese, ⅓ cup sultanas and 2 teaspoons honey in small bowl. Heat a small greased heavy-based frying pan. Pour 2 tablespoons batter into pan, tilting pan to coat base; cook crêpe until browned lightly. Brown crêpe on other side; remove from pan, cover to keep warm. Repeat with remaining batter. Place rounded tablespoons of ricotta mixture in centre of crêpes; roll to cover filling, fold in sides, then roll to enclose filling.

prep + cook time 40 minutes (+ standing) **makes** 8

nutritional count per crêpe 5.5g total fat (3.3g saturated fat); 573kJ (137 cal); 14.9g carbohydrate; 6.3g protein; 0.6g fibre

tips Serve crêpes dusted with icing sugar. You could use frozen ready-made crêpes, or freeze your own, if you like. The filling needs to be made on the day of serving. Honey may contain harmful bacteria and is not recommended for children under one year old.

poached pear rice pudding

Combine 1 litre milk and ¼ cup caster sugar in medium saucepan; bring to the boil, stirring occasionally. Gradually stir in ⅓ cup medium-grain washed and drained white rice; simmer, uncovered, stirring occasionally, about 40 minutes or until rice is tender. Meanwhile, combine 2 cups water, 1 small peeled, halved pear and 1 cinnamon stick in small saucepan; bring to the boil. Simmer, uncovered, about 25 minutes or until pear is tender. Remove pear from liquid, chop finely; reserve 2 teaspoons, stir remaining pear into pudding. Top with reserved pear. Serve warm.

prep + cook time 1 hour **serves** 6

nutritional count per serving 6.6g total fat (4.3g saturated fat); 853kJ (204 cal); 29g carbohydrate; 6.5g protein; 0.8g fibre

tip Sprinkle with a pinch of ground cinnamon. The rice pudding can be made a day ahead, or frozen in serving sized portions for up to a month. You can use canned pears in natural juice instead of fresh pears.

poached pear rice pudding

rhubarb, apple and pear crumble

ricotta and honey crêpes

stocks

These recipes can be made up to 4 days ahead; refrigerate overnight then remove any fat from the surface. Keep stock, covered, in the refrigerator. All the recipes make approximately 2.5 litres (10 cups).

fish stock

1.5kg fish bones

3 litres (12 cups) water

1 medium onion (150g), chopped coarsely

2 stalks celery (300g), chopped coarsely

2 bay leaves

1 teaspoon black peppercorns

1 Combine ingredients in large saucepan; bring to the boil. Reduce heat; simmer, uncovered, about 20 minutes.

2 Strain into large heatproof bowl; cool then refrigerate.

prep + cook time 30 minutes (+ refrigeration)

nutritional count per cup (250ml) 0.2g total fat

(0.1g saturated fat); 63kJ (15 cal); 1g carbohydrate; 1.9g protein; 0.8g fibre

vegetable stock

2 large carrots (360g), chopped coarsely

2 large parsnips (700g), chopped coarsely

4 medium onions (600g), chopped coarsely

10 stalks celery (1.5kg), chopped coarsely

4 bay leaves

2 teaspoons black peppercorns

6 litres (24 cups) water

1 Combine ingredients in large saucepan; bring to the boil. Reduce heat; simmer, uncovered, about 1½ hours.

2 Strain into large heatproof bowl; cool then refrigerate.

prep + cook time 1 hour 40 minutes (+ refrigeration)

nutritional count per cup (250ml) 0.3g total fat

(0g saturated fat); 276kJ (66 cal); 11.6g carbohydrate; 2.4g protein; 3.8g fibre

beef stock

2kg meaty beef bones

2 medium onions (300g), chopped coarsely

2 stalks celery (300g), chopped coarsely

2 medium carrots (240g), chopped coarsely

3 bay leaves

2 teaspoons black peppercorns

5 litres (20 cups) water

3 litres (12 cups) water, extra

1 Preheat oven to 220°C/200°C fan-forced.

2 Place bones and onion in baking dish. Bake about 1 hour or until well browned.

3 Transfer bones and onion to large saucepan, add the celery, carrot, bay leaves, peppercorns and the water; bring to the boil. Reduce heat; simmer, uncovered, 3 hours. Add the extra water; simmer, uncovered, about 1 hour. Strain into large heatproof bowl; cool then refrigerate.

prep + cook time 5 hours 30 minutes (+ refrigeration)

nutritional count per cup (250ml) 0.6g total fat

(0.2g saturated fat); 134kJ (32 cal); 2.8g carbohydrate; 2.9g protein; 1.7g fibre

chicken stock

2kg chicken bones

2 medium onions (300g), chopped coarsely

2 stalks celery (300g), chopped coarsely

2 medium carrots (240g), chopped coarsely

3 bay leaves

2 teaspoons black peppercorns

5 litres (20 cups) water

1 Combine ingredients in large saucepan; bring to the boil. Reduce heat; simmer, uncovered, about 2 hours.

2 Strain into large heatproof bowl; cool then refrigerate.

prep + cook time 2 hours 10 minutes (+ refrigeration)

nutritional count per cup (250ml) 0.9g total fat

(0.3g saturated fat); 146kJ (35 cal); 3.2g carbohydrate; 2.7g protein; 1.5g fibre

glossary

allspice also known as pimento or jamaican pepper; available whole or ground. Tastes like a blend of cinnamon, clove and nutmeg – all spices.

baking powder a raising agent that aerates and lightens mixtures during baking. Also available as gluten-free.

beans
borlotti also known as roman beans or pink beans because they are pale pink or beige with dark red streaks. Available fresh or dried.
butter also known as lima beans; large, flat, kidney-shaped bean, off-white in colour, with a mealy texture and mild taste. Available canned and dried.
mexe-style (mexican-style) a mildly-spiced canned combination of kidney or pinto beans.

beetroot also known as red beets or just beets; firm, round root vegetable.

bicarbonate of soda also known as baking or carb soda; a leavening agent used in baking.

bread
french stick bread that's been formed into a long, narrow cylindrical loaf. It is also known as french bread, french loaf or baguette.
fruit loaf contains sultanas and other dried fruits and spices.
par-baked partially-baked bread only needing a few minutes in the oven to give fresh-baked rolls. Available from most supermarkets.
pitta also known as lebanese bread. Sold in large, flat pieces that separate into two thin rounds. Also available in small thick pieces called pocket pitta.
tortilla thin, round unleavened bread originating in Mexico; available made from either wheat flour or corn.
turkish also known as pide; comes in long (about 45cm) flat loaves as well as individual rounds.

buk choy, baby also known as pak kat farang or shanghai bok choy; is much smaller and more tender than buk choy.

buttermilk originally the term given to the slightly sour liquid left after butter was churned from cream, today it is made similarly to yogurt. Sold alongside all fresh milk products in supermarkets. Despite its name, it is low in fat.

capsicum also known as bell pepper or, simply, pepper. Discard seeds and membranes before use.
roasted available loose from delis or packed in jars in oil or brine.

cheese
cherry bocconcini walnut-sized, fresh, baby mozzarella, a delicate, semi-soft, white cheese. Spoils rapidly, so must be kept under refrigeration, in brine, for one or two days at most.
cottage fresh, white, unripened curd cheese with a grainy consistency.
cream commonly known as Philly or Philadelphia, a soft cows-milk cheese. Also available as spreadable light cream cheese, which is a blend of cottage and cream cheeses.
soya made from soy extract and selected cultures.

chervil also known as cicily.

chicken
drumsticks has skin and bone intact.
drumettes small fleshy part of the wing between shoulder and elbow, trimmed to resemble a drumstick (leg).
tenderloins thin strip of meat lying just under the breast.

chorizo a sausage of Spanish origin, made of coarsely ground pork and highly seasoned with garlic and chillies.

coriander also known as pak chee, cilantro or chinese parsley; bright-green leafy herb with a pungent flavour. Both stems and roots are used in cooking; wash well before using. Also available ground or as seeds; these should not be substituted for fresh coriander as the tastes are completely different.

cornflakes cereal made of dehydrated then baked crisp flakes of corn. Also available finely ground and is used for coating or crumbing food.

cornflour also known as cornstarch; used as a thickening agent in cooking. Available made from 100% corn as well as wheat. Wheaten cornflour gives cakes a lighter texture (due to the fact it has some gluten).

cornichons French for gherkin, a very small variety of cucumber.

couscous a fine, grain-like cereal product made from semolina; from the countries of North Africa. A semolina flour and water dough is sieved then dehydrated to produce minuscule even-sized pellets of couscous; it is rehydrated by steaming, or with the addition of a warm liquid, and swells to three or four times its original size.

cucumber, lebanese short, slender and thin-skinned. Probably the most popular variety because of its tender, edible skin, tiny, yielding seeds, and sweet, fresh and flavoursome taste.

cumin also known as zeera or comino.

dairy-free spread (dairy-free margarine) commercially made margarine, free of dairy products.

eggs if recipes in this book call for raw or barely cooked eggs, excercise caution if you are at risk of salmonella food poisoning (pregnant women, young children and those suffering from immune deficiency diseases).

eggplant purple-skinned vegetable also known as aubergine. Also available char-grilled, packed in oil, in jars.
baby also known as finger or japanese eggplant; very small and slender.

fish fillets, firm white any boneless firm white fish fillet – blue eye, swordfish, bream, ling, whiting or sea perch are all good choices. Check for any small pieces of bone in the fillets and use tweezers to remove them.

flour
buckwheat not a true cereal, but a flour that is made from its seeds. Available from health-food stores.
chickpea also called besan or gram; made from ground chickpeas so is gluten-free and high in protein. Available from health-food stores and most supermarkets.
plain an all-purpose flour made from wheat. Also available as gluten-free from most supermarkets.
rice, white very fine, almost powdery, gluten-free flour; made from ground white rice.
rice, brown retains the outer bran layer of the rice grain; it has a slightly chewy texture and a nut-like flavour.
self-raising plain flour mixed with baking powder in the proportion of 1 cup flour to 2 teaspoons baking powder. Also available as gluten-free from most supermarkets.
soya made from ground soya beans.

gelatine we used powdered gelatine. It is also available in sheet form, known as leaf gelatine.

kecap manis *see sauces, soy.*

kitchen string made of a natural product such as cotton or hemp so it neither affects the flavour of the food it's tied around nor melts when heated.

kumara Polynesian name of orange-fleshed sweet potato often confused with yam.

lamington pan 20cm x 30cm slab cake pan, 3cm deep.

malted milk powder a combination of wheat flour, malt flour and milk, which are evaporated to give the powder its fine appearance and to make it easily absorbable in liquids. Delicious when mixed with warm milk; may also be used to add a malted flavour in baking.

maple syrup a thin syrup distilled from the sap of the maple tree. Maple-flavoured syrup or pancake syrup is not an adequate substitute for the real thing.

Milo sweetened chocolate malted milk drink base.

muesli also known as granola.

noodles, hokkien also known as stir-fry noodles; fresh noodles resembling thick, yellow-brown spaghetti.

onion
green also known as scallion or, incorrectly, shallot; an immature onion picked before the bulb has formed, having a long, bright-green edible stalk.
red also known as spanish, red spanish or bermuda onion; a sweet-flavoured, large, purple-red onion.

parsley, flat-leaf also known as continental or italian parsley.

pepitas dried pumpkin seeds.

polenta also known as cornmeal; a flour-like cereal made of dried corn (maize) sold ground in different textures. Also the name of the dish made from it.

potatoes, baby new also known as chats; not a separate variety but an early harvest with very thin skin.

prawns also known as shrimp.

preserved lemon rind quartered lemons are preserved in salt and lemon juice or water. To use, remove and discard pulp, squeeze juice from rind then rinse rind well and slice thinly. Sold in jars or singly by delicatessens; once opened, store under refrigeration.

prosciutto a kind of unsmoked Italian ham; salted, air-cured and aged, it is usually eaten uncooked.

puffed millet the smallest of all grains, millet has been cultivated for thousands of years. It has a mildly sweet, nut-like flavour. Puffed millet is steamed then heated until it puffs up, similar to puffed rice cereals.

puffed rice a type of puffed grain made from rice; usually made by heating rice kernels under high pressure in the presence of steam.

raisins dried sweet grapes.

rice bubbles puffed rice cereal.

rice flakes dehusked rice flattened into flat light dry flakes, which swell when added to liquid. The thicknesses vary between almost translucently thin (the more expensive varieties) to nearly four times thicker than a normal rice grain.

rice paper sheets also known as banh trang. Made from rice paste and stamped into rounds. Are quite brittle and will break if dropped; dipped momentarily in water they become pliable wrappers for fried food and uncooked vegetables. Make good spring-roll wrappers.

rocket also known as arugula, rugula and rucola; a peppery-tasting green leaf. Baby rocket leaves (wild rocket) are both smaller and less peppery.

rockmelon also known as cantaloupe and musk melon.

rolled oats oat groats (oats that have been husked) steamed-softened, flattened with rollers, dried and packaged for consumption as a cereal product.

sambal oelek (ulek or olek) Indonesian in origin; a salty paste made from ground chillies and vinegar.

sauces
barbecue a spicy, tomato-based sauce used to marinate or as a condiment.
fish also called nam pla or nuoc nam; made from pulverised salted fermented fish, most often anchovies. Has a pungent smell and strong taste. so use according to your taste.
hoisin a thick, sweet and spicy Chinese paste made from salted fermented soya beans, onions and garlic.
mint made from finely chopped fresh mint leaves, soaked in vinegar and a small amount of sugar.
plum a thick, sweet and sour dipping sauce made from plums, vinegar, sugar, chillies and spices.
satay spicy peanut sauce served with grilled meat skewers.
soy made from fermented soya beans. Several variations are available in most supermarkets and Asian food stores.
japanese soy an all-purpose low-sodium soy sauce made with more wheat content than its Chinese counterparts; fermented in barrels and aged. Possibly the best table soy and the one to choose if you only want one variety.
kecap manis (ketjap manis) a thick soy sauce with added sugar and spices.
light soy a fairly thin, pale but salty tasting sauce; used in dishes where the natural colour of the ingredients is to be maintained. Not to be confused with salt-reduced or low-sodium soy sauces.
sweet chilli a comparatively mild, Thai-style sauce made from red chillies, sugar, garlic and vinegar.
tomato also known as ketchup or catsup; a condiment made from tomatoes, vinegar and spices.
tomato pasta made from a blend of tomatoes, herbs and spices.
worcestershire a dark coloured condiment made from garlic, soy sauce, tamarind, onions, molasses, lime, anchovies, vinegar and seasonings. Available in most supermarkets.

shallots also called french shallots, golden shallots or eschalots; small, brown-skinned, elongated members of the onion family.

soy milk a rich creamy 'milk' extracted from soya beans that have been crushed in hot water and strained. It has a nutty flavour. Sometimes malt and barley extract are added to soy milk to make it more palatable. Ensure you use gluten-free soy milk if you have a gluten allergy.

spinach also known as english spinach and, incorrectly, silver beet.

squid hoods also known as calamari; a type of mollusc. Buy squid hoods to make preparation and cooking easier.

sugar
brown soft, finely granulated sugar retaining molasses for its characteristic colour and flavour.
caster also known as superfine or finely granulated table sugar.
icing also known as confectioners' sugar or powdered sugar; granulated sugar crushed together with a small amount of added cornflour.
pure icing also known as confectioners' sugar or powdered sugar, but has no added cornflour.
white a coarse, granulated table sugar, also known as crystal sugar.

sultanas dried grapes, also known as golden raisins.

sunflower seed kernels dried husked sunflower seeds.

sweetened condensed milk from which 60% of the water has been removed; the remaining milk is then sweetened with sugar.

veal schnitzel a thinly sliced steak available crumbed or plain (uncrumbed); we use plain schnitzel, sometimes called escalopes, in our recipes.

Vegemite Australia's favourite spread. A dark brown food paste used on toast and sandwiches. Made from leftover brewers' yeast extract, the taste may be described as salty, slightly bitter and malty. The texture is smooth and sticky.

vinegar
balsamic a deep, rich, brown vinegar with a sweet and sour flavour. Made from the juice of Trebbiano grapes.
cider (apple cider) made from fermented apples. Can be alcoholic or non-alcoholic.
white wine made from white wines.

wombok also known as peking cabbage, chinese cabbage or petsai. Elongated in shape with pale green, crinkly leaves.

wonton wrappers also known as wonton skins. Sold in the refrigerated section of Asian grocery stores and supermarkets; gow gee, egg or spring roll pastry sheets can be substituted.

zucchini also known as courgette.

conversion chart

measures

One Australian metric measuring cup holds approximately 250ml; one Australian metric tablespoon holds 20ml; one Australian metric teaspoon holds 5ml. The difference between one country's measuring cups and another's is within a two- or three-teaspoon variance, and will not affect your cooking results. North America, New Zealand and the United Kingdom use a 15ml tablespoon.

All cup and spoon measurements are level. The most accurate way of measuring dry ingredients is to weigh them. When measuring liquids, use a clear glass or plastic jug with the metric markings.

We use large eggs with an average weight of 60g.

dry measures

METRIC	IMPERIAL
15g	½oz
30g	1oz
60g	2oz
90g	3oz
125g	4oz (¼lb)
155g	5oz
185g	6oz
220g	7oz
250g	8oz (½lb)
280g	9oz
315g	10oz
345g	11oz
375g	12oz (¾lb)
410g	13oz
440g	14oz
470g	15oz
500g	16oz (1lb)
750g	24oz (1½lb)
1kg	32oz (2lb)

liquid measures

METRIC	IMPERIAL
30ml	1 fluid oz
60ml	2 fluid oz
100ml	3 fluid oz
125ml	4 fluid oz
150ml	5 fluid oz (¼ pint/1 gill)
190ml	6 fluid oz
250ml	8 fluid oz
300ml	10 fluid oz (½ pint)
500ml	16 fluid oz
600ml	20 fluid oz (1 pint)
1000ml (1 litre)	1¾ pints

length measures

METRIC	IMPERIAL
3mm	⅛in
6mm	¼in
1cm	½in
2cm	¾in
2.5cm	1in
5cm	2in
6cm	2½in
8cm	3in
10cm	4in
13cm	5in
15cm	6in
18cm	7in
20cm	8in
23cm	9in
25cm	10in
28cm	11in
30cm	12in (1ft)

oven temperatures

These oven temperatures are only a guide for conventional ovens. For fan-forced ovens, check the manufacturer's manual.

	°C (CELSIUS)	°F (FAHRENHEIT)	GAS MARK
Very slow	120	250	½
Slow	150	275-300	1-2
Moderately slow	160	325	3
Moderate	180	350-375	4-5
Moderately hot	200	400	6
Hot	220	425-450	7-8
Very hot	240	475	9

index

If you like this cookbook, you'll love these...

These are just a small selection of titles available in
The Australian Women's Weekly range on sale at selected
newsagents, supermarkets or online at www.acpbooks.com.au

also available in bookstores...

ACP BOOKS

General manager Christine Whiston

Editor-in-chief Susan Tomnay

Creative director Hieu Chi Nguyen

Art director & designer Hannah Blackmore

Contributing writer Elizabeth Wilson

Food director Pamela Clark

Test Kitchen manager + nutritional information Belinda Farlow

Recipe development Mary Wills, Amal Webster, Peta Dent

Food preparation Rebecca Squadrito, Nicole Jennings

Sales & rights director Brian Cearnes

Marketing manager Bridget Cody

Senior business analyst Rebecca Varela

Circulation manager Jama Mclean

Operations manager David Scotto

Production manager Victoria Jefferys

ACP Books are published by ACP Magazines a division of
PBL Media Pty Limited

PBL Media, Chief Executive Officer Ian Law

Publishing & sales director, Women's lifestyle Lynette Phillips

Group editorial director, Women's lifestyle Pat Ingram

Marketing director, Women's lifestyle Matthew Dominello

Commercial manager, Women's lifestyle Seymour Cohen

Research director, Women's lifestyle Justin Stone

Produced by ACP Books, Sydney.

Published by ACP Books, a division of ACP Magazines Ltd,
54 Park St, Sydney; GPO Box 4088, Sydney, NSW 2001.
phone (02) 9282 8618; fax (02) 9267 9438;
acpbooks@acpmagazines.com.au; www.acpbooks.com.au

Printed by Toppan Printing Co, China.

Australia Distributed by Network Services,
phone +61 2 9282 8777; fax +61 2 9264 3278;
networkweb@networkservicescompany.com.au

United Kingdom Distributed by Australian Consolidated Press (UK),
phone (01604) 642 200; fax (01604) 642 300; books@acpuk.com

New Zealand Distributed by Netlink Distribution Company,
phone (9) 366 9966; ask@ndc.co.nz

South Africa Distributed by PSD Promotions,
phone (27 11) 392 6065/6/7; fax (27 11) 392 6079/80;
orders@psdprom.co.za

Canada Distributed by Publishers Group Canada
phone (800) 663 5714; fax (800) 565 3770; service@raincoast.com

Title: Food for healthy babies and toddlers / food director
Pamela Clark.
ISBN: 978 186396 902 4 (pbk.)
Notes: Includes index.
Subjects: Cookery (Baby foods) Children-Nutrition.
Other Authors/Contributors:Clark, Pamela.
Dewey Number: 641.56222
© ACP Magazines Ltd 2009
ABN 18 053 273 546

Scanpan cookware is used in the AWW Test Kitchen.

To order books, phone 136 116 (within Australia)
or order online at www.acpbooks.com.au
Send recipe enquiries to:
recipeenquiries@acpmagazines.com.au